fit
for
GOLF

Gary Player

WEIDENFELD & NICOLSON
London

First published in Great Britain in 1994
by Weidenfeld & Nicolson
The Orion Publishing Group Ltd
Orion House
5 Upper St Martin's Lane
London WC2H 9EA

Copyright © 1994 by Gary Player

Typeset by Superskill Graphics Pte. Ltd.
Reproduction by Sixty-Six Lithographic
Pte. Ltd.
Printed in Singapore by CS Graphics
Pte. Ltd.

ISBN 0 297 83404 5

IF YOU HAVE ANY DOUBTS ABOUT YOUR ABILITY
TO PERFORM THE ACTIVITIES DESCRIBED IN THIS
BOOK, OR IF YOU HAVE A MEDICAL CONDITION,
FIRST SEEK THE OPINION OF A QUALIFIED MEDICAL
PRACTITIONER. THE AUTHOR AND THE PUBLISHER
CANNOT ACCEPT RESPONSIBILITY FOR INJURY OR
DAMAGE SUFFERED BY ANY PERSON ATTEMPTING
THE ACTIVITIES DESCRIBED HERE. ALL WARNINGS
AND GUIDELINES SHOULD BE READ CAREFULLY.

Contents

Foreword

Gary Player is truly a sporting phenomenon of our times. His success in the golfing arena has made him one of the most recognized and admired figures in the history of the game, his achievements having assured him of a permanent position in the golfing hall of fame. But what are the real reasons behind his remarkable success? What are the methods by which Gary not only has reached the pinnacle of his chosen sport, but remained there in a feat of consistency and endurance that few have been able to emulate to this day?

I have tried to find answers to these questions whenever Gary and I have been brought together throughout our friendship after our common interest in fitness and nutrition led to our acquaintance some twenty years ago. Like any successful person, Gary has a set of guidelines and principles to which he adheres, and which provide the foundation for his accomplishments. One comment comes to mind that I think sums up the essence of his success. Referred to frequently as ambassador of golf, Gary confided to me, 'I would rather be known as an ambassador for fitness'.

Of course, I was impressed. There was a man who at the prime of his success, had a larger goal in life than collecting trophies and titles. He wanted and still wants to win others over to a healthy lifestyle by practising what he preaches. His highly disciplined exercise and nutritional regimen which founded his fame and fortune mean more to him than a means to an end and became an end in its own right.

This book is another testimony to Gary's lifelong commitment to the promotion of physical fitness. He has combined his first-hand knowledge of golf, fitness and nutrition into a valuable manual for all golfers who want to play or live better.

Kenneth H. Cooper

Kenneth H. Cooper, M.D.

Introduction Unfit persons

may think they have a better chance of performing well in golf than in any other sport. Fairways, tee-boxes and driving ranges all over the world abound with flabby arms, bulging waistlines and double chins. Such shapes seem to stick out more on the tennis court, in the boxing ring or in the swimming pool. But even if you have never dreamed of attempting anything more strenuous than a nine-hole round on a Sunday morning, your golf performance suffers from too sedate a lifestyle.

If you are overweight, it becomes all too easy to adopt a poor posture at address. Instead of standing up to the ball with the back straight, and the arms hanging from the shoulders, you're likely to stand too erect, with the hands too far from the body, or reach for the ball too much with a convex curve of the back. This stance puts too much weight on the heels or toes.

Either way, you're off balance, and your legs won't function properly during the swing. Worse, a big belly tends to put the lower spine in an unnatural, concave position. This is because, whether standing or walking, most overweight people tend to thrust the tummy forward to balance themselves more easily. Such poor posture can lead to back problems.

But even if you are slim, without regular exercise, the agility, strength and coordination so necessary in golf will suffer, your swing will shorten, and you won't hit the ball as far.

If only golfers realize that time and effort spent exercising at home or in the gym actually helps to reduce the score out on the course. By training the correct muscles you can easily increase the strength and coordination you need for a powerful golf swing.

Don't get me wrong, mere muscle doesn't turn a hacker into a good golfer, just as mere technical skill doesn't make a pro. But it takes a fit, flexible body, with strong muscles, elastic tendons and endurance to put the basic knowledge and understanding of the golf swing to best use. Fitness separates the fumbler from the golfer.

Without my life-long commitment to fitness, I would not have achieved half as much as I did as a golfer, a father or a businessman. I would not have had the stamina to travel as many miles or win as many trophies in major tournaments, against the likes of Arnold Palmer and Jack Nicklaus.

I knew that if I were ever to become a champion professional golfer I would have to work at it, harder than the average man, for my size, a mere 5 foot 7 inches, and weight, 145 pounds, were both against me.

To build up my legs I ran. My brother Ian always went with me, up and down the dusty gold mine hills of South Africa. When I wanted to quit, breathless and feeling rather weak after a mile or so, he wouldn't let me. Because of Ian I came to realize that I could keep going when I thought I couldn't. Over the years I've made a lot of money in golf by not giving up when the going got rough, and when it looked like there was no chance of winning. There are many professional players out there saying: 'If I can't win this tournament, I don't care if I'm out of the money.' But I'd rather finish 40th than 50th and I'd rather win $100 than $10.

To build my arms, I did push-ups – with Ian standing over me counting. In those days I did 70 fingertip push-ups, spread throughout a day, trying to build up my thin arms and fragile fingers, because fitness for golf extends right to the fingertips. A favourite trick of mine, which demonstrates this, is to balance a heavy club, held horizontal between index and forefinger, without using my thumb for support. Try it for yourself, and you'll find out how challenging it is.

Even then, I found while practising for the 1960 U.S. Masters that I couldn't reach the par five's on my second shot like the other top players. When I spoke to Peter Thomson about it he told me he didn't believe he could ever win the Masters because he was such a short hitter, and like me, couldn't reach the long holes in two.

I learned the hard way that just hard work alone doesn't do the trick. I needed professional advice to train the right muscles in my body to get where I wanted. So I hired a professional body builder who started me on weight exercises, while I continued my push-ups and endurance exercises. A year later I won the Masters.

That year, a U.S. magazine ran a survey on just where the drives landed. Figures showed that my tee shots ended very close to Arnold Palmer's! And in 1965 at Augusta I had the best score of the field on the par five's, even beating the winner, Jack Nicklaus, by one stroke, on these holes that once were too long for me.

Today, at 58, I've retained the length of swing from my early years, and I can still hit the ball much the same distance. Because I do stretching exercises, I'm not sore after a round. Because I've kept my legs in good shape and because exercises build and strengthen the bones, I can still use the wider stance of a young man.

I have no problem getting my weight back and through the ball. I can walk a hilly course, and not be breathless as I come up the 18th hole. My energy level is high. And I actually weigh less now as a Senior Tour player than at the peak of my career.

I know that when I'm fit, my reflexes and touch are better, my eyesight is sharper, as is my hearing. Just as important, my brain is clearer and my concentration is keener.

Although getting started on my fitness discipline has been one of the hardest decisions in my life, it is now my lifestyle of choice. I prefer a banana and a handful of raisins to a hearty meal, hundreds of push-ups to a movie and water to wine. I have done and still do all this, simply because I continue to enjoy the rewards.

Of course, I don't expect you to follow in my footsteps. You may have little or no inclination for an active fitness schedule, or even the slightest intention of winning the U.S. Masters.

But if you are serious about reducing your handicap, or beating the hell out of your foursome partners next month, this book may be for you. If all those useful magazine articles, books and lessons on the mechanics of the swing don't bring the results you're looking for, start your individual fitness programme.

In this book I am not trying to put you through a daunting *tour de force,* Gary Player-style. There are probably as many different levels of fitness as there are styles of playing golf, and I believe you should play and exercise your way.

I will show you a wide variety of different exercises meant to increase your flexibility, strength, endurance and coordination on the fairway. After having gone through a test to determine which of your golfing muscles need attention, you put your own routine together, consisting of basic and optional exercises. When you have mastered those, you may want to experiment with the advanced training.

Get those flabby arms, those waistlines and double chins under control, and put more power into your swing. And don't start tomorrow, start today. Start by walking up those stairs to your office instead of taking the elevator, by skipping a rope at lunchtime or by riding a stationary bicycle next to your bath tub

while the water is running. I promise you,
it will work wonders on your swing.

If you follow my advice and work out
regularly, you will

- hit further because your muscles
  become stronger

- hit more consistently because your
  stamina increases

- improve your swing because your
  body rotates better

- get rid of ingrained swing faults
  because you will be more supple

- improve your feel and muscle
  memory

- swing longer and faster because you
  have more oxygen in the body

- risk less injury through bad posture

What are you waiting for?

The Golf Swing

To improve your performance on the golf course through fitness training, you need to understand not only the fundamental technique of the swing but also which parts of the body are involved in the mechanics of it. Whether you hit a long drive, or make a short putt, all movements are brought by the muscles which shorten or lengthen across the different types of joints in the body. The muscles are attached to the bones through tendons, and ligaments hold the joints in place when the muscles move. Let's look in detail at the coordination of upper and lower body, the contraction and extension of muscles and tendons, the twisting and turning of joints and bones.

THE MUSCLES

Since muscles originate movement, their importance for the golf swing cannot be overemphasized. It goes far beyond the mere mechanics. The golf swing is essentially a question of feel. In other words, how the player perceives the motion through the muscles. Obviously, the better trained the muscles are, the more accurate the feedback you receive from them. This basic truth gains more importance with age, as the muscle structure begins to degenerate once you are past 30.

You have undoubtedly heard of

muscle memory. Actually, this is a contradiction in terms. A muscle cannot memorize anything at all. However, all muscle movement is initiated by and memorized in the brain. The more often a certain movement is performed, the clearer its image in the brain becomes. This, in turn, triggers a fast automatic muscle response when the movement is performed next. In other words, the more you practise your swing, the better your chance of performing it more consistently in the future.

This consistency is an ideal standard that professionals try to achieve through endless swing training, and which is probably mastered best by Nick Faldo today. Lesser professionals often struggle to maintain the same swing over the years, and amateurs frequently lose their swing during a single round.

Muscle memory is primarily a matter of exercise. It can be learned and unlearned. It appears that strengthening exercises shorten the information lag between brain and muscle. A sensible training programme will also improve the consistency of your swing throughout a round by boosting your endurance, as your muscles won't tire easily any more.

In an age where distance off the tee has become almost an obsession with most professionals and amateur players, quite a number of golfers appear to believe that distance results from strong arm muscles. This is not so. The power of a muscle is directly related to the size of its cross-section. So no matter how strong your arms are, they can't compete with your legs.

To generate the momentum necessary to deliver arms, hands and the club to the ball speedily, accurately and forcefully, the biggest muscles in the body are employed: the extensors and abductors of the hips, which in turn move the hip backward and straighten it. The hip actually initiates the downswing and is the driving force at impact. You have to exercise your hip muscles and use them effectively during your swing to gain that distance off the tee.

At address, you initially use the straight abdominals, a set of four muscles, which bend the torso forward. The knee flexors, commonly called *hamstrings,* bend the knee slightly, while the ankle dorsiflexors and plantarflexors have lifted and pointed the toes to correct the stance. The eractor spinae keeps the back straight. The neck flexors have tilted your head forward at address. The chest muscle, pectoralis major, has pulled the arms in front of the body. The elbow extensors have straightened your elbow, the wrist extensors the wrists, and the numerous and minuscule muscles in the fingers enable you to get a good grip of the club.

During the backswing, the knee flexors remain bent, but also start to rotate, once the hip abductor has initiated the rotation of the right hip. The hip flexor moves the left hip forward. The oblique externals, flanking the waistline, pick up the rotary movement and turn the torso. The plantarflexors relax a little on the left ankle, which straightens slightly, when you lift your heel during the backswing, but remain pretty much in place for the right ankle.

The most important role for the shoulder rotation is played, according to the findings of the Centinela Hospital Medical Center in California, by the rotator cuff muscles, a set of four lying between the deltoid and the shoulder joint. While I always thought that the large deltoid was responsible for the arm movement during the swing, the researchers established that the smaller rotator cuffs actually did most of the work of turning the shoulders backward and forward and swinging the arms back. Biceps and triceps in the arm assist in rotating the arms and protecting the shoulder joint during the backswing.

The trapezius at the base of the skull turns the left shoulder blade outward, while the broad back muscle, the latissimus dorsi swings the right arm backward and rotates the left arm inward. The elbow flexor slightly bends your right elbow, and, to a lesser extent, the left, while the wrist flexors bend both wrists. At this stage it is easy to understand that with so many muscles involved the small finger muscles holding on to the club are by now often forgotten. Novice golfers especially tend to relax the grip which is a very common swing mistake.

On the downswing the entire concerted muscle action is reversed. Where the extensor operated, the flexor picks up, and vice versa. And during the follow-through, the action of most muscles used during the downswing is mirrored on the left side of the body. The above-mentioned researchers were also able to determinc that the golf swing is really a balanced action involving both sides of the body to an equal extent. This should surprise advocates of a stronger left side.

This, mind you is a very rough sketch of the fine-tuned interaction of a multitude of muscles during the swing, but it should be sufficient to explain to you which areas you may wish to work on to improve your game. Before we put our sweat shirts on, let's take a brief look at the bones during a golf swing. The bones are prone to suffer most from wear and tear if joints and ligaments are not flexible and even from injuries if untrained muscles build up ingrained swing faults.

THE BONES

The golf swing is performed by coiling the upper body on the back swing against the resistance of the lower body before being unleashed. This means that powerful muscles twist and pull at the lumbar spine. Due to a bad posture, poor back and abdominal toning and inflexibility, the discs of the spine may be squeezed during the swing and lower back trouble can result. Stretching and strength exercises can help you to maintain or regain your suppleness and empower the muscles to actively cushion the blow.

It is the bones which benefit most from

exercise as you grow older. Without training they become brittle and fragile and tend to break easily. But even with all the exercise my bones have received throughout the years, as I approached 40 I began looking for an alternative to the traditional golf swing. The reverse C-shape of the spine in the follow-through demands the flexibility and strength of a young golfer which I no longer had.

I started to emulate the old heroes of the game like James Braid, Walter Hagen and Gene Sarazen. They all had lasted way past their prime on the tour by employing a much gentler swing, without sacrificing their scoring skills.

A young golfer keeps arms and hands passive during the backswing, so that the clubface is closed at the top, and depends on the rotation of the body to deliver the clubface at the correct angle to the ball. I now open the clubface by rolling the hands to the right early in the backswing and close it by rolling the wrists towards the left in the downswing. So I achieve the same effect without putting any strain on the spine.

Like these great players, I often find myself walking after the ball with this new swing almost as though I had lost balance. But this only shows that I actually made the right weight transfer and executed the stroke well with the ball perfectly on line. I now can hit the ball as hard and as long as before – and win a few championships along the way – without putting additional stress on a physique that was beginning to need more care.

Today, older players such as Raymond
Floyd, Hale Irwin, Jack Nicklaus and
myself have proven the success of a swing
gentle enough to last a lifetime. Amateur
golfers, who often play well into their old
age, can only benefit from these
experiences by enjoying better rounds of
golf than ever before and beating their
age with their score.

Fitness Test

Stamina, flexibility, coordination and power mainly determine your performance on the golf course, but regardless of your current level of fitness you will possess each of these qualities to a different degree. In order for your game to benefit quickly from your exercise efforts you need to pinpoint your areas of greatest weakness. So before you plunge headlong into your training session, take a little time for our fitness test. Grab a pen and paper to record your results as you'll need them later for reference. You may want to repeat the test as you proceed with your exercise routine to check your progress.

This is a test for all golfers, young and old, small, tall, heavy, slight, male or female. Since ladies are generally at least as flexible as men, everybody gets the same points for the same performance in the flexibility test. However, in the strength test the scoring system differs for the sexes. If you are a very young or very old golfer, or someone who has had ill health, you may want to compare your score with those of the ladies rather than the men. And do check with your physician before starting the test if you have not exercised regularly before.

T E S T   R E S U L T S

Date					
FLEXIBILITY					
Calf Stretch					
Torso Stretch					
Lateral Bends					
STRENGTH					
Thigh Power					
Upper Body Strength					
Stomach Strength					
STAMINA					
The Cooper Test					
TOTAL					

FLEXIBILITY

The ability to twist the upper body against the lower body is one of the most important factors for a solid golf swing, but there are many more areas where flexibility is needed in golf. You need to be supple to bend the upper body at address and to stretch and rotate the legs and hips during the swing. You need to lean your back backward during the follow-through – even though I do not advocate the reverse-C position – and you need to turn your upper body sideways for better weight transfer. Let's find out how well you can do it.

1. Calf Stretch

Place a ruler next to a piano leg, a cupboard, chest or pillar in your house.

Fitness Test

CALF STRETCH

Inches	Points
–1"	1
0"	2
1"	3
2"	4
3"	5
4"	6
5"	7

Sit down on the floor with stretched legs and place the sole of your feet against the aforementioned piece of furniture. Align the zero of the ruler to where your feet meet the obstacle in extension of your legs. Bend your upper body forward and try with your fingers to reach your toes or beyond. The ruler indicates the points you gain as shown on the right.

2. Torso Stretch

Ask your wife or a friend to assist you with this one. Lie down next to a wall on your stomach with your arms stretched and joined at your back. Your partner picks up the ruler and marks the height of your shoulder blades with a pencil on the wall. Now you raise your upper body without straining your neck and ask your partner to mark the position of the shoulder blade on the wall again. Then you stand up and measure the results, that is, the distance between the two dots on the wall. Give yourself one point for each inch. Maximum is seven points. But don't let your partner run off just yet.

3. Lateral Bends

LATERAL BENDS

Inches	Points
2"	1
4"	2
6"	3
8"	4
10"	5

You stand upright with your back against the wall and let your arms drop with your palms facing the body. Ask your partner to mark on the wall with a pencil where your palms end. Now move one hand down along the body towards the floor by keeping your head and shoulders firmly pressed against the wall. Ask your partner to mark again and measure the distance. Repeat the procedure with the other hand. A differential of about one inch between the results for each hand is considered normal. Pick your favourite side, but give yourself points only for that side as shown on the previous page.

TORSO TURNS

4. *Torso Turns*

Angle	Points
15°	1
30°	2
45°	3
60°	4
75°	5
90°	6

You need a golf club for this test and an objective judge (your partner perhaps), if you have a tendency to cheat. Sit upright in a chair with your back leaning against the backrest. Place the club across both shoulders and wrap your arms around the club from the back so that elbow joints and shoulders are aligned to hold the club in place. Let your hands dangle down in front. Twist your torso first to one side as far as you can while keeping your back straight. Give yourself points according to the angle between your maximum reach and your original position.

STRENGTH

The powerful swing is a result of the tension between the strength of your upper thighs, which balances your legs and lower body, and the twisting forces of the rotating upper body. If the muscles in your thighs are not well-trained, your golf swing will at best be weak, and at worst throw you off balance. The oblique externals, which are similarly a powerful force in rotating the body, determine in principle the arch of your swing. If they are weak your swing becomes short and static. Strength is also sorely needed in your chest and shoulder muscles, as well as in your triceps to generate enough speed at impact.

1. *Thigh Power*

Warning: Refrain if you have a history of knee trouble.

Stand upright with your back against a wall, your feet about thigh's length in front of you. Bend your knees and slide down along the wall with your back firmly pressed against the wall until your knees are bent at 90°. Remain in this position as long as possible and count the seconds you are able to do so.

THIGH POWER

MEN		WOMEN
Sec	Points	Sec
20	1	12
30	2	18
40	3	24
50	4	30
60	5	36
70	6	42
80	7	48

2. *Upper Body Strength*

While young and strong men should stick to the usual push-up position where only hands and toes are allowed to touch the floor, seniors and ladies may rest on hands and knees. The hands should be positioned shoulder-width apart with fingertips pointing in front. Count how many push-ups you can do in 30 seconds, but make sure your chest has touched the floor each time.

PUSH-UP

MEN		WOMEN
Repetitions	Points	Repetitions
5	1	3
10	2	6
15	3	9
20	4	12
25	5	15
30	6	18
35	7	21

STOMACH STRENGTH

MEN		WOMEN
Repetitions	Points	Repetitions
30	1	20
35	2	25
40	3	30
45	4	35
50	5	40
55	6	45
60	7	50

4. Stomach Strength

Warning: Refrain if you suffer from back pain.

Sit down on the floor with knees bent, facing a wall. Rest your upper body on the floor and walk up the wall with your legs until your feet are in line with your knees. Fold your arms up behind your head and sit up with a slight twist until your right elbow touches your left knee. Return your torso to the floor at least until your shoulder touches it and repeat for the other side. Count how often you can repeat the sit-ups each side within one minute.

STAMINA

Although a number of people believe that golf is really a sedate past-time for the aged and decrepit, or even a good walk ruined, you and I know that it takes a lot of stamina to walk four hours of often severely graded terrain and to hit the ball with a powerful, even swing for maximum impact some seventy or more times throughout a round.

The level of endurance depends in principle on how much oxygen your lungs can handle and how fast your heart can pump this oxygen into the blood stream.

1. The Cooper Endurance Test

Warning: Refrain if you have heart trouble.

This is basically the outdoor version of the treadmill which you may have come across during your medical check-ups.

You can either measure how much time it takes you to run 1.5 miles or how far you can run within 12 minutes. Alternatively, you can count the number of times you can skip a rope or how many steps you can climb up and down during this period.

OVERALL RESULTS

0–10 POINTS

You're out of shape in a bad way! Your overall fitness level, or rather the lack of it must drive your physician to distraction. One advantage, of course is that starting from a zero base you stand to gain the most from your exercise programme – on and off the fairways. But before you embark on a fitness programme please check with your doctor. With his or her approval start slowly with the basic exercises which you can manage to do, and cut down on the number of repetitions if you must.

11–20 POINTS

You probably like to potter about in your garden, go fishing or have active grandchildren as I do who keep you from falling asleep in front of the TV set. Your fitness score is slightly below average, but you are promising fitness-material to work on, with ample room for improvement. Start to develop your own programme by sticking to the basics first. As your fitness level increases, you may want to repeat the test and expand your routine to concentrate on areas where you perform below average.

ENDURANCE TEST

MEN		
1.5 Miles	Points	12 Minutes
16:00 min	1	2200 y
14:00 min	2	2420 y
12:00 min	3	2640 y
10:45 min	4	2860 y
9:45 min	5	3080 y

WOMEN		
1.5 Miles	Points	12 Minutes
21:00 min	1	1540 y
19:30 min	2	1760 y
17:30 min	3	1980 y
16:00 min	4	2200 y
14:30 min	5	2420 y

21–30 POINTS

Not bad at all. You have an average fitness level. Keep up the good work, and don't let your strength and stamina deteriorate. You want to look carefully into the individual test results to single out those areas where you most need improvement. When it comes to putting your own training routine together, you may expand the basic routine by selecting from the optional and advanced exercises.

31–39 POINTS

Congratulations! You are a fitness buff like me. You have your exercise routine firmly in place and have been working out regularly. You want to improve your game? To do so, double-check that you have all the basic exercises incorporated into your workout and pick from the optional and advanced category those exercises for areas of shortcomings.

RECOGNIZE YOUR WEAKNESSES

Now that you have ascertained your current fitness level, I want you to look at your results for each of the six test exercises individually. How did you fare?

0–2 POINTS

For an exercise indicates a physical weakness for you, which you can overcome through training. If you have not exercised before, the basic exercises should improve your overall performance as well as results in your problem area. If

26

your general fitness level is average or above, an individual bad result highlights a potential trouble spot, which you may have overlooked before. Concentrate on this specific area by selecting exercises from our optional, or if you are really very fit, advanced category, to correct the situation.

3–5 POINTS

Indicate an average performance, which you need to maintain and probably want to improve. You don't want to remain an average golfer all your life, do you? Work on these areas specifically through the selection of optional exercises, but only as and when your overall performance in our fitness test is average or better, otherwise our basic workout will take care of the problems.

6–7 POINTS

Per test exercise prove that all you really need to do is maintain your level of performance. The basic exercises will do this nicely. However, as your overall performance improves, you may want to look into the advanced exercises to expand or vary your routine. Since I get bored easily, I usually follow a routine until my body gets used to it, then I introduce some variations and surprise it a bit. You must, however, ensure that your exercise schedule caters for all parts of the body. In other words, you must revert to the basic exercises regularly.

FITNESS TIPS

- walk whenever you can

- climb stairs where possible

- cycle if you can

- play tennis

- go swimming

- get into horseback riding

- buy a jump rope

- go dancing

- try yoga

- venture into cross-country skiing

- exercise with music

- if you skip training today, get back to it tomorrow

- vary your workout

The Exercises

Fitness relates first to health and second to performance. As golfers, we are interested in the latter, but without the basics we would not be able to perform. Consequently, this book is divided into basic exercises to improve your overall health and fitness by working on your cardiovascular endurance, your muscle stamina and body flexibility, and optional exercises to improve your golf performance, emphasizing coordination, muscle strength and speed. The specific advanced performance-related exercises are reserved for very fit people.

To make this book easy to follow the basic exercises for the flexibility, calisthenics and power plan are marked with bright, solid colour. The optional ones are slightly lighter in tone and the advanced exercises are outlined in pastels. The exercises are organized in the sequence they should be performed, starting with the big muscles of the body first, your chest, then your legs, followed by your arms to avoid physical injury. Warm-up and cool down sessions are essential at the beginning and end of each workout.

To get you started on your way to becoming a better golfer, here are some easy tips to get more activity, energy and health out of your daily life. I believe that they will not only turn you into a better player on the course, but will also benefit your business performance.

28

Before you plunge into your individual exercise schedule, you should look carefully at the list of cautionary guidelines.

My 1-hour workout is rather strenuous:

1.   Stretching in the hot bath
2.   Cold shower
3.   Additional stretching
4.   Swing heavy club
5.   Stationary bicycle
6.   Additional stretching
7.   Sit-ups with 50 pounds
8.   Lunges with 50 pounds
9.   Toe raises
10. Push-ups
11. Leg raises
12. Reverse arches
13. Neck exercises
14. More stretching
15. Hand exercises
16. Swing heavy club
17. Stair machine
18. Stationary bicycle

WARNINGS

- don't exercise without checking with your physician

- don't exercise when you have an infection

- don't exercise before or right after meals

- don't drink alcohol when you exercise

- don't snack while exercising

- drink water, even if you are not (yet) thirsty

- pain means injury – stop exercising and see a doctor

Warming Up

Every exercise session, regardless of how fit you are, must start with warming up. If you owned a high performance motor car you would hardly race the engine without making sure it was warmed up first. Considering the complexity of the human body it is no wonder that a lack of warm up before any exercise or a round of golf can lead to tears – of both kinds!

Warming up, as the name suggests, increases the temperature of the body and speeds up the heart rate and blood circulation preventing strains on muscles, tendons, ligaments, joints, lungs and the heart. This ensures that you and your body are physically and mentally prepared for any vigorous workout.

A warm-up consists of a combination of exercises. You start slowly with stretching all the joints in your body. Stretching has actually become an integral part of my life since it not only sets me up for physical exercise, but also helps to avoid strain and stress during the day.

You may want to stretch after waking up in the morning, while sitting at your desk, after standing all day and every time you feel stiff, tight or tense.

When you stretch, make sure that you are relaxed. Take it easy, breathe slowly and deeply. Don't force the movement, don't bounce, and don't compare yourself to others. This is not the time to get competitive.

Whether you do it in the morning, during your office lunch break or before a

WARNINGS

- Your knees should always be slightly bent

- Do not lock arms and legs

- Do not rotate the neck

- Do not overstretch the back

- Do not bend over for long periods

round of golf, a warm-up session should include stretching, the use of a static bicycle, a light jog or brisk walk, pauses to shake or massage your limbs, and should last about ten minutes.

Especially if you haven't exercised before, you should pay attention to the warnings opposite.

Gary Player

HEAD ROLL

Stand upright, move the head from side to side while keeping the shoulders still. Repeat slowly five times each side.

SHOULDER ROLL

Stand upright. Hold a
club in both hands and
pull the shoulders up,
back and down without
bending the arms. Keep
a constant rolling action.
Repeat five times.
Reverse by rolling
shoulders upward in the
opposite direction.
Repeat five more times.

BACK EXTENSION

Stand upright. Hold a club in both hands and raise the club with extended arms above the head. Squat down with a stretched back and lean slightly forward. You should create an extended line with arms, head and back. Repeat five times.

33

BACK STRETCH

Squat down, holding a
club in both hands, and
place it on the knees.
Keep the back straight.
By tilting the head
slightly down start to
round the back into a
comfortable position and
hold. Return to starting
position without
overstretching the back.
Repeat six times.

Warming Up

SHOULDER
ROTATION

Hold a club in both hands and place it on the knees. Squat down to a comfortable position. Keep the head and back aligned while turning alternative shoulders forward. Lead the action with bent elbows. Repeat six times each side.

Note: Keep the head still, rotate around the vertebral column.

35

WAIST TWIST

Stand upright with the knees slightly bent. Hold a club in both hands and start rotating to both sides. Keep the head and knees still moving only the trunk. Twist to a comfortable range. Arms can be slightly flexed or extended.

Note: Do not move the knees when twisting.

36

SIDE REACH

Stand upright, keeping the knees slightly flexed and take a club in both hands. Bend the waist and stretch with the club to each side in a controlled rhythmic action keeping the head still. Repeat six times each side.

WINDMILL

Stand upright with knees slightly bent while holding a club in both hands. Lean forward with a straight back. Turn to the side and move until you stand upright again. Turn to the opposite side and back to the starting position. Maintain a smooth, controlled circular action. Repeat five times and reverse directions.

Note: Keep knees bent. Do not bend backwards. Come up to an upright position and do not bend too far forward.

FLOOR REACH

Stand upright with
slightly flexed knees,
holding a club in one
hand. Bend in the waist,
turning to one side and
place the club on the
floor, reaching out as far
as possible. Repeat six
times each side.

MARCHING

Stand upright with slightly flexed knees, holding a club in both hands. Raise arms and knees simultaneously in a rhythmic manner. Keep the back straight. Exhale and inhale rhythmically. Repeat ten times each side.

SIDE SHOULDER PRESS

Stretch the shoulder from the waist to each side with a club held in both hands above the shoulders. Squat slightly. Repeat ten times each side.

SIDE SHOULDER PRESS WITH TAPS

Stretch the shoulder again from the waist to each side with a club held in both hands above the shoulders. Perform single taps with the opposite foot. Repeat ten times each side.

ARM ROTATION

Stand upright, holding a club in both hands vertically in front of you. Squat down while turning the club clockwise. Stand up by returning the club to its original position. Now turn the club counter-clockwise while squatting again. Repeat ten times.

CALF STRETCH

This exercise can prevent achilles tendon tears by stretching the heel. Place a golf club on the floor so that you can toe the line. From a standing position bend over while keeping both feet together. Keep the head and back still and alternate by pushing the heels onto the floor with a rhythmic action. You should feel the stretch in your rear leg. Repeat ten times each leg.

Note: Do not maintain this bent over position for long periods.

INNER THIGH STRETCH

Place a golf club on the ground. Space your hands out to a comfortable position on the club and bend one leg while stretching the other. Keep the back and neck straight. Move from side to side with slow, controlled actions. Pause in the middle if you need a breather.

Note: Do not squat too low down on the one leg, and do not stretch too far.

Stretching

Since the golf swing involves power, speed and intensive twisting of the body at the same time, flexibility training is probably the most important part of your daily routine. Supple muscles, tendons and ligaments work better and are less prone to injuries. Without flexibility training your muscles will shorten over time and so will your swing.

You can gain agility by stretching a certain joint up to a position which you can maintain for ten seconds or so. You must be careful to move very gently and slowly to reach the maximum muscle elongation, and your body will tell you very clearly when to stop. This method of training is quite strenuous, as all you really do is straightforward stretching. You'll no doubt feel it.

For good measure you'll find on the next pages dynamic elasticity exercises as well, involving fast movements, rotations and swings with golf clubs. You'll probably find that the momentum generated by clubs and body during so much action helps you to stretch further for a short time, but without the slow exercises, the effect of the flexibility training would be incomplete.

If you're just starting out on flexibility training, take it easy and don't try to achieve too much too fast. Concentrate rather on getting the exercises right. To start with you may want to ask your partner to check on you or work with a mirror in front of you. Remember also to repeat each exercise at least six times on each side.

NECK STRETCH

This is a good way to start your stretching routine. Stand up looking straight ahead. Place one hand behind the head and stretch the other down next to the body. Slowly pull the head to the side while pushing the stretched arm down. Hold for six to twelve seconds and repeat. Switch sides.

CHEST-SHOULDER-BACK STRETCH

Place both hands behind the back. Interlock the fingers with the palms facing upward and elbows facing inwards. Stretch your arms. Hold. Repeat.

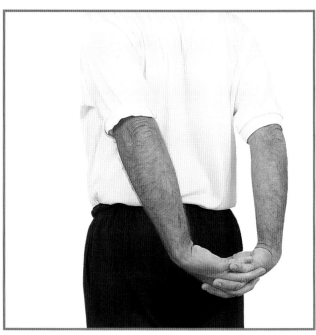

**B A S I C
E X E R C I S E S**

STANDING QUADRICEPS STRETCH

Stand upright and hold onto a chair or any other suitable object for balance with one hand. Pull the heel of one leg up to the buttocks with the other hand and feel the quadriceps in the front of the upper thigh stretch. Bend the other leg slightly to reduce the stress of the lower back. Switch sides.

HIP FLEXOR STRETCH

Stand upright and put one leg on the seat of a chair or bench. Both feet must be aligned. Keep a straight back and place both hands on the knees for support. Hold. Repeat with the other leg.

STANDING HAMSTRING STRETCH

Stand with one leg resting on a chair, allowing the other to bend naturally to maintain your balance. Hold on to the stretched leg for support and slide your hands down the leg feeling the stretch. Breathe in on the way down and breathe out when you get to your limit. Keep the hands on the leg for support. Repeat with the other leg.

Note: Do not force the head down.

SPINAL TWIST

Sit on a chair and point both feet straight ahead. Slowly turn the upper body around and place both hands at waist-height on the back rest. Hold for eight seconds. Release the grip and turn slowly back to a normal sitting position. Repeat on the opposite side.

BENT-OVER SHOULDER STRETCH

Sit on a chair and interlock your fingers behind the back. Stretch your arms, bend over and pull the arms slowly up and over the back.

LATERAL SHOULDER STRETCH

Crouch on the knees at a comfortable distance from a chair. Place both hands on the seat of the chair with your arms stretched out. Keep the head between the arms. Push down from the shoulder and feel the latissimus dorsi stretching on the downward movement.

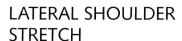

B A S I C
E X E R C I S E S

ELONGATION STRETCH

Lie on your back. Stretch the arms over the head with your legs out straight. Try to reach out as far as is comfortable with both arms and legs. Hold for ten seconds and relax.

SINGLE KNEE-TUCK

The exercise stretches the lower back, the hip extensors and the hamstrings, and helps to prevent injuries in this area. Lie down on your back. Breathe in and pull one knee onto the chest with both hands, keeping the other leg stretched. Bring the head up to meet the knee and breathe out. Hold for eight seconds. Return to the original position and change legs. Repeat six times each side.

TRUNK TWIST

The flexibility of the spine is very important for the golf swing. Lie on your back and stretch out your arms at shoulder height on the floor. Bend the legs and bring them up onto the chest. The higher you pull your knees up to your chest, the more you will stretch the spine. Breathe in and turn both legs, with knees bent, towards the side until they make contact with the floor, while keeping your arms and shoulders still on the floor. Breathe out and relax. Hold for eight seconds. Breathe in, pull the knees up and return to your original position. Breathe out and relax. Repeat six times. Switch sides.

Note: Do not do this movement with straight legs and keep the knees as close to the chest as possible.

**B A S I C
E X E R C I S E S**

CAT STRETCH

Go down on all fours. Keep the back straight. Breathe in. Pull the head in, contract the stomach muscles and round the back as far as is comfortably possible and breathe out. Hold for eight seconds and return to the original position.

BACK STRETCH

Place both hands behind the back. Interlock the fingers with the palms facing outwards and elbows facing inwards. Stretch arms. Hold. Repeat.

OPTIONAL EXERCISES

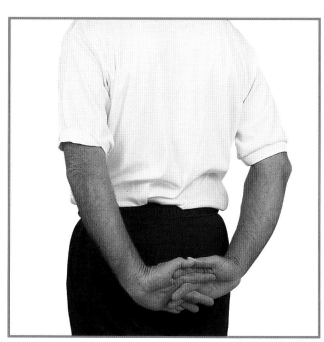

STANDING HAMSTRING STRETCH

Keep one leg bent, holding onto the stretched leg for support. Lean forward from the hips with an extended back position. Inhale on the way down and exhale when reaching your own personal maximum range. Inhale to support the back.

Note: Do not force the head down.

HIP FLEXOR STRETCH

Squat down with your palms on the floor in front of you. Bend your knees by 90°. Keep the rear leg straight in line with the back and neck. Rest the trunk on the bent leg. Change legs and repeat six times.

DOUBLE KNEE-TUCK

Lie down on your back. Breathe in and pull your knees with both hands onto the chest. Bring the head up to meet the knees and breathe out. Hold for eight seconds. Return to the original position.

QUADRICEPS STRETCH

Lie down on your stomach and place the forehead onto one arm. Take hold of the foot with the other hand. Pull the heel towards the buttocks with a slow, controlled action and hold for a count of eight seconds. Change legs and repeat.

Note: Keep the head down.

OPTIONAL
EXERCISES

SEATED GROIN STRETCH

Sit down and place the soles of the feet against each other. Hold onto the feet with the hands and stretch the elbows. Start in an upright position. Breathe in, then slowly lean down towards the feet. Breathe out and relax. Hold for eight seconds. Breathe in and return to the original position. Breathe out.

TRICEPS PULL

Hold a club in both hands behind the back. Keep one arm extended with the hand placed on the clubhead and bend the other arm behind the head holding onto the grip of the club. Push down with the straight arm and feel the triceps stretch with the upper flexed arm. Hold for eight seconds and repeat with the other arm.

SHOULDER STRETCH

Squat down and place your hands on the floor behind your back with your fingers pointing towards your feet and your legs comfortably apart. Slowly push forward with the knees so that the stretch can be felt on the shoulder.

Note: Do not remain in this position for too long.

ADVANCED EXERCISES

DOUBLE KNEE-TUCK

Lie down on your back and bring the hands together underneath both knees. Breathe in and pull the knees onto the chest, while holding onto the elbows. Bring the head up to meet the knees and breathe out. Hold for eight seconds.

SEATED HAMSTRING STRETCH

Sit down on the floor with one leg stretched and the other bent against your thigh, while keeping it as close to the floor as possible. Place your hands on the extended leg and slide them down on the leg while inhaling. Breathe out when you reach your limit. You should feel the pull behind the knee. Work the other side. Repeat six times each.

Note: Do not force the head down.

SEATED BACK STRETCH

Sit down with both legs stretched out. Cross one leg over the other. Sit up straight, breathe in and swivel the trunk, placing one arm on the floor beside your leg and the other arm on the floor behind your back. Breathe out and relax in that position. Hold for eight seconds. Breathe in, turn forward slowly with the trunk and breathe out. Change leg and arm positions and repeat.

FOREARM STRETCH

Kneel down, place your hands on the floor with the fingers pointing towards the knees. Keep your palms flat while gently stretching the forearms. Hold for eight seconds.

ADVANCED EXERCISES

Skill Toning

The most difficult task that every novice golfer faces is pulling all the different parts of the swing together and keeping them there. This demands the cooperation of an incredible variety of large and minute muscles and joints through feel and tempo. Beginners often attempt to memorize too much and end up confused. Or they concentrate on one particular aspect of the swing and forget to perform the rest. Coordination is the name of the game.

To get your golf muscles and joints to work together, you want to use muscle memory. The coordination workout focuses on a variety of movements which occur during the golf swing. You can do some of the exercises easily in your office, at home or on the driving range. Apart from the exercises involving golf clubs, you don't even need a warm-up to start.

You can follow this drill four to five times a week, but not before a tournament, and don't exceed half an hour each time. Allow for breaks of 30 seconds between exercises. To get the most out of the skill toning workout, you will have to take a heftier volume for the book exercises, increase the weight of the club and the number of clubs respectively in your exercises. You will also have to swap the rubber ball for one made of a denser material.

BOOK LIFT

To train your hands, wrists and forearms, indispensable in your connection with the golf club throughout the entire swing, hold a fairly large book between the palms. Stretch the arms forward and roll the wrists up and down with the book firmly in place. Repeat 20 times. Change to a heavier volume as you progress.

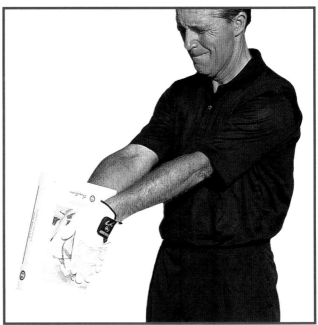

FOREARM ROTATION

Hold a fairly large book between the palms. Stretch the arms forward and rotate the forearms to the left and then to the right side. This exercise will do wonders for your forearms and biceps if you repeat it 20 times.

CLUB LIFT

After you have gone through a proper warm up, paying special attention to the lower back, hold a heavy club in one hand in the normal address position. Lift the club until the clubhead is pointing towards the sky. Try to maintain your normal swing arch. This is a good exercise for your wrist and biceps. Repeat 20 times or so until your arm becomes tired. Switch sides and do another 20.

WRIST ROTATION

Hold a heavy club in one hand. Lift the clubhead off the ground and move the clubhead in small circles. Increase the circles until you feel the strain in the wrist and forearm. Repeat 20 times. Switch sides and do another 20.

SWING A HEAVY CLUB

Swing a heavy club like a right-handed golfer and then like a left-handed golfer. Make sure you maintain your normal swing to develop your golf muscles on both sides. Repeat 20 times each side. If you have no heavy club readily available take two normal ones instead.

LEFT ARM SWING

Grip a heavy club with the left hand only. Imitate your golf swing by swinging with your left arm only for about 20 times. Repeat with right arm.

GRASS CUTTING

Grass Cutting strengthens all golf muscles. Swing continuously with the wedge in high or rough grass about 20 times. Eventually, you may want to take a longer club.

TENNIS BALL SQUEEZE

Hold a tennis ball in the palm of the hand and squeeze it repeatedly with the fingers. To train fingers and forearms, repeat 20 times in each hand. As you get stronger, switch to a ball of higher density.

WEIGHT WINDING

You need a strong string of roughly one yard length, a stick or walking cane and a full ball bag or a bucket of golf balls or stones. Tie the golf ball bag firmly to the middle of the cane. Take both ends of the cane in your hands, stretch the arms forward and wind up the string on the pole by twisting it in your hands until the weight reaches the pole. If this appears too cumbersome a contraption to build, such equipment can also be bought. Repeat 20 times to condition forearms and shoulders. As you perform better, increase the rolling speed of the weight.

WEIGHT-TRANSFER

To improve your
weight-transfer
performance on the
course, pick your sport
of choice and try to
emulate the actions in
the photographs. You
will see that the weight
transfer necessary in
sports like karate,
baseball, boxing, tennis,
or even casting a fishing
line, is similar to that in
the golf swing.

Calisthenics

The golfer's ability to swing the club consistently well throughout an entire round depends on stamina, that is the endurance power of the golf muscles. Calisthenics are the best way to increase your stamina because they increase your oxygen level and heart beat and train your muscles to make the most out of this sudden supply of reserves (oxygen and blood).

Ideally, you should do calisthenics twice or three times a week for about 20 to 30 minutes. Rest for 15 seconds in between exercises. Throughout the entire calisthenics session you must monitor your heart rate and keep it well below 180 beats per minute.

Do the basic exercises until you get comfortable with them. Only then may you try out the optional drill. The advanced exercises are reserved for very fit persons. Before you start on any of the exercises you must first go through the warm-up.

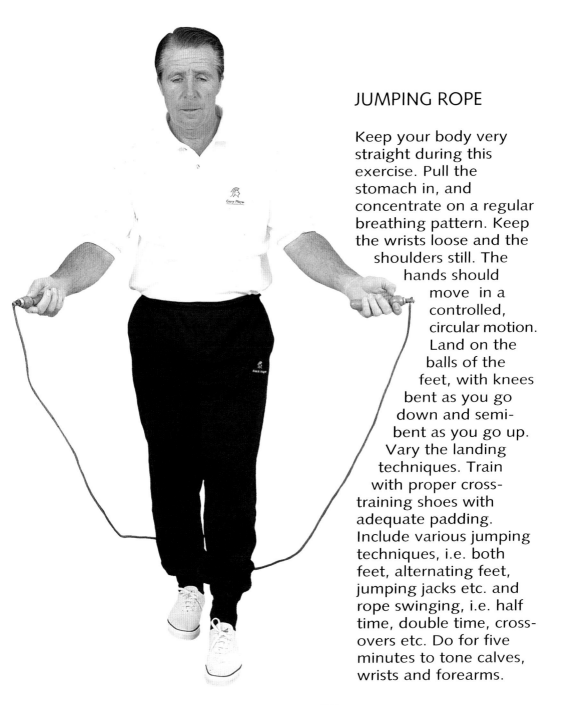

JUMPING ROPE

Keep your body very straight during this exercise. Pull the stomach in, and concentrate on a regular breathing pattern. Keep the wrists loose and the shoulders still. The hands should move in a controlled, circular motion. Land on the balls of the feet, with knees bent as you go down and semi-bent as you go up. Vary the landing techniques. Train with proper cross-training shoes with adequate padding. Include various jumping techniques, i.e. both feet, alternating feet, jumping jacks etc. and rope swinging, i.e. half time, double time, cross-overs etc. Do for five minutes to tone calves, wrists and forearms.

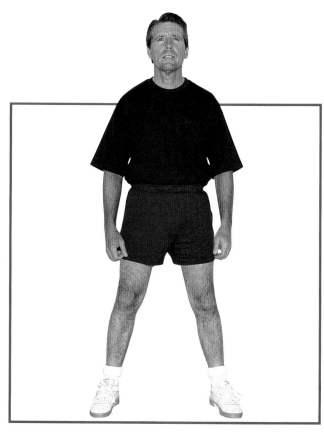

WALL SQUAT

This exercise strengthens the quadriceps and helps stabilize your golf swing. Stand upright and press the back flat against the wall and slide down until your knees are at a 90° angle and remain in this position. Keep the arms folded in front with the elbows up. Hold. Repeat ten times.

**B A S I C
E X E R C I S E S**

Calisthenics

SIT-UP

Lie on your back with the knees bent, head up and chin forward, looking towards the ceiling with the lower back pressed against the floor. Pull yourself up to 30–40° and breathe out. Return to the original position with the head and shoulders off the ground. You should feel the pull in the abdominals. Repeat 20 times.

PELVIC LIFT

This exercise will do wonders for your lower back. Lie on your back and keep the head down. Place your arms next to your sides. Tilt the pelvis up keeping the lower back in contact with the floor. You will feel the stomach muscles contracting. Hold for ten seconds and lower the pelvis again. Repeat ten times.

PUSH-UP

To give your triceps, deltoids and chest a good workout, go down on all fours and place your hands in front of the shoulders, with your fingers pointing forward just more than shoulder-width apart. The back and neck should be in a straight line. Cross the legs behind the buttocks with your feet in the air. Breathe in and lower your chest almost to the floor. Do not over-stretch the back. Push back to the original position and breathe out. Repeat 20 times.

Note: Do not lock the elbows, but keep them slightly bent.

B A S I C
E X E R C I S E S

UPPER BODY STRETCH

Lie down on your stomach and place both arms underneath the forehead. Breathe in as you lift your upper body from the floor keeping the legs stationary on the floor. Return to the original position and breathe out. Repeat ten times.

Note: Do not look up.

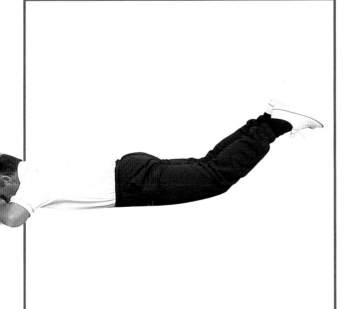

LOWER BODY STRETCH

Lie down on your stomach and place your arms underneath the forehead. Breathe in as you lift the lower limbs keeping the upper body stationary on the floor. Repeat ten times.

Note: Do not look up.

OPPOSITE ARM AND LEG EXTENSION

This is a great strengthening exercise for the extensors in the back. Lie down on your stomach and stretch out the body. Lift your right arm and left leg to a comfortable position while breathing in. Return to the original position while you breathe out. Switch to the other side. Repeat ten times.

**B A S I C
E X E R C I S E S**

TWIST SIT-UP

Lie on your back and cross the legs. Lift them in the air by 90° with the knees bent. Keep the lower back pressed on the floor and your knees level with the chest. Place your hands behind the head or fingers on the temples. Twist your waist and touch the knee with the opposite elbow. Repeat ten times.

OPTIONAL EXERCISES

ALTERNATING LEG STRETCH

This is a great exercise for the hip flexors, buttocks and thighs. Squat down. Place your hands on the floor for support and bring your feet together with the hips remaining above the shoulders. Stretch one leg back. Return to your original position and alternate the action with the other leg in a smooth manner. Repeat ten times.

BURPEES

Stand upright and lift
your arms in the air.
Squat down with your
palms flat on the floor
and then kick out both
legs behind, keeping
your hips up higher than
your shoulders. Bring
back both legs together
to the squat position
and repeat ten times.

OPTIONAL
EXERCISES

LEG STRETCH
SIT-UP

Lie on your back and keep the legs bent and together pulling the knees up in line with the hips. Keep your chin forward, shoulders off the floor and the hands behind the head. Stretch the legs and come up with the upper body. Touch the toes and breathe out. Return to the original position by lowering the upper body and legs. Repeat ten times.

A D V A N C E D
E X E R C I S E S

ALTERNATE BENT KNEE JACKKNIFE

This is another great way to train your abdominals. Lie on your back and place the hands behind the head with the chin forward. Keep one leg on the floor, always bent. Lift the opposite leg, slightly bent, towards the chest and simultaneously come up with the upper body and breathe out. Alternate this exercise with a smooth, controlled motion. Repeat ten times.

PUSH-UP

Go down on all fours and place your hands in front of the shoulders, with your fingers pointing forward, just more than shoulder-width apart. Raise the hips slightly and keep the neck and back in line throughout the whole movement. Breathe in and lower your chest almost to the floor. Do not over-stretch the back. Push back to the original position and breathe out. Repeat 20 times.

ADVANCED EXERCISES

Calisthenics

TRICEP DIP

Squat and place your hands on the floor behind you, palms facing forward, with your bottom raised off the ground and your feet firmly on the floor. Bring one leg up in the air and stretch it while keeping the other foot on the floor. Keep the stomach muscles contracted, chin up and breathe as you lower yourself down with the elbows slightly flexed. Without touching the floor bring yourself back up to the original position, and breathe out. Repeat ten times.

- Do every exercise very slowly after having stretched your muscles first. Start with the basic exercises beginning with the large muscle groups. Repeat every exercise six times. And don't forget to do your warm-up first.

- Strength training must be progressive. You have to increase the number of repetitions or the load every time you workout. However, your strength improves significantly only when you increase the load you are working with.

- Do not workout every day. Three times a week is an optimum to build up strength. To maintain your strength once a week is enough. Your muscles need time to recover.

Power Plan

Hitting a golf ball repeatedly and repeatedly well and accurately takes strength and endurance. Strengthening your golf muscles will not only increase the speed of your swing and the force applied to the ball at impact, to send the ball further, but will also improve your posture. It may even help to prevent and cure back pains by cushioning the forces pulling at the vertebral column during the swing. I know that because I have tried it.

To strengthen a muscle, it has to be subjected to tension by lengthening or shortening it. Moving a weight such as dumbbells will accomplish this. The weight you are struggling against determines how much power you have to apply. Initially, choose a weight which you can lift easily, somewhere between two to five pounds. As you progress, you should increase the load to about ten to 15 pounds. The weight will feel heavier or lighter than it actually is depending on what you do with it.

On the left you find a few guidelines to keep in mind when you want to strike the ball with more power and consistency by increasing your muscle power.

MEDIAL ROTATIONS

The pectoralis major, the large muscle in your chest, is instrumental in lifting the club and hitting the ball at impact. To train it, stand upright, holding a dumbbell in each hand, and let the arms hang next to your sides with the palms facing forward. Turn the dumbbells in towards your body so that your palms are facing outwards, and hold the contraction for five seconds. Repeat ten times.

LATERAL RAISE

Sit upright in a chair. Hold a dumbbell in each hand at the side of the body. Lift the dumbbells up to the level of your shoulders keeping your elbows slightly bent and breathe out. Slowly lower the dumbbells without losing complete tension and breathe in again. Repeat ten times.

B A S I C
E X E R C I S E S

SEATED SHOULDER PRESS

This is a good way to exercise your deltoids. Sit in a chair with a dumbbell in each hand at shoulder-level with palms facing inwards. Push both dumbbells out and up with a twisting movement as you breathe out. The movement ends with extended arms and palms facing inwards. Don't extend your arms all the way. Breathe in when returning to the starting position. Repeat ten times.

DOUBLE BICEPS CURL

Sit upright in a chair. Place the elbows at your sides and the dumbbells at shoulder-level. Lower the dumbbells without straightening your arms completely. Breathe in. Bring the dumbbells back to a starting, flexed position and breathe out. Maintain a steady rhythm. Repeat ten times.

B A S I C
E X E R C I S E S

TRICEPS STRETCH

Sit upright in a chair. Hold a dumbbell with both hands and place it on the upper back. Extend the elbows and feel the dumbbell rising up. Breathe out. Keep elbows still. Lower the dumbbell down the back and breathe in. Repeat ten times.

FRONT RAISES

Sit upright in a chair. Keep your elbows slightly bent, palms facing downward. Breathe regularly while alternately lifting the arms, preventing the dumbbells from touching the knees. Repeat ten times.

OPTIONAL EXERCISES

Power Plan

BARBELL SQUAT

To train your quadriceps, hamstrings and buttocks, place the barbell on your shoulders. Stand with your feet comfortably apart, the toes pointing slightly outwards. Inhale on the way down and keep the back slightly extended. Do not go lower than 90°. Come up to the starting position and exhale.

Note: Concentrate on your straight back position.

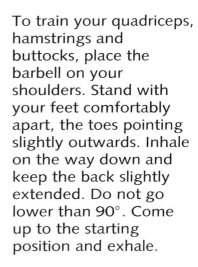

CLEAN AND PRESS

This is a good exercise for quadriceps, hamstrings, deltoids and the back. Stand up straight and raise the barbell up to a position just in front of the shoulders. Breathe in. Lower the barbell to a point below the bent knees while keeping the head up. Straighten up by pulling the barbell up to shoulder height. Immediately press the barbell out above the shoulders and prevent overstretching of the back. Breathe out. Lower the barbell onto the shoulders. Relax. Repeat five times.

OPTIONAL EXERCISES

WRIST FLEXION

Sit on a chair. Hold on to a barbell with both hands resting on the lap with palms down and the wrists just off the knees. Turn the wrists slightly upwards and then downwards. Do the movement slowly and with control. Repeat ten times.

OPTIONAL EXERCISES

WRIST EXTENSION

Strengthening your forearm muscles and wrists will help you to control the club during the swing and to prevent the clubhead from wobbling. Sit on a chair. Hold onto a barbell with both hands resting on the lap with palms up and the wrists just off the knees. Bend the wrists upwards then downwards over the knees. Do the movement slowly and with control. Repeat ten times.

LUNGE

To train quadriceps, hamstrings and buttocks, stand upright and hold a barbell shoulder-high behind your neck. Place the hands a comfortable distance apart to maintain balance. Keep the head up. With one leg stretched behind, bend your knee, but no more than 90°. Avoid touching the floor with the rear knee. Breathe in on the way down and breathe out at the end of the push-off phase. Repeat ten times.

A D V A N C E D
E X E R C I S E S

SEATED SHOULDER PRESS

Sit in a chair with a dumbbell in each hand at shoulder-level with palms forward. Push both dumbbells out and up as you breathe out. Don't extend your arms all the way. Breathe in when returning to the starting position. Repeat ten times.

WRIST EXTENSION

Sit on a chair. Hold on to a barbell with both hands resting on the lap, palms up. Extend the wrist upwards then let the barbell roll down the hands into the fingers. Curl the wrist upwards and repeat the same action. Do the movement slowly and with control. Repeat ten times.

ADVANCED EXERCISES

Cooling Down

It is as imperative to cool down after exercising as it is to warm-up beforehand. Strenuous training can build up stress chemicals in the blood which may endanger the heart. You cannot cool down by simply turning on the cold shower. On the contrary, you can only do so after you have cooled down properly. A very simple way of cooling down is walking or bicycling as I do.

The exercises you will find below are part of the stretching routine and have proved very effective in easing tension after a long golf practice, and I use them after every workout. The deep breathing that should accompany the stretching exercises calms and cools the body, and, if done properly, replenishes the energy for tasks ahead.

NECK STRETCH

This is a good way to start your stretching routine. Stand up looking straight ahead. Place one hand behind the head and stretch the other down next to the body. Slowly pull the head to the side while pushing the stretched arm down. Hold for six to twelve seconds and repeat. Switch sides.

CHEST-SHOULDER-BACK STRETCH

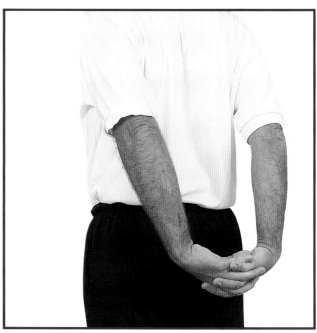

Place both hands behind the back. Interlock the fingers with the palms facing upward and elbows facing inwards. Stretch your arms. Hold. Repeat.

Cooling Down

STANDING QUADRICEPS STRETCH

Stand upright and hold onto a chair or any other suitable object for balance with one hand. Pull the heel of one leg up to the buttocks with the other hand and feel the quadriceps in the front of the upper thigh stretch. Bend the other leg slightly to reduce the stress of the lower back. Switch sides.

HIP FLEXOR STRETCH

Stand upright and put one leg on the seat of a chair or bench. Both feet must be aligned. Keep a straight back and place both hands on the lifted knee for support. Hold. Repeat with the other leg.

STANDING HAMSTRING STRETCH

Stand with one leg resting on a chair, allowing the other to bend naturally to maintain your balance. Hold on to the stretched leg for support and slide your hands down the leg feeling the stretch. Breathe in on the way down and breathe out when you get to your limit. Keep the hands on the leg for support. Repeat with the other leg.

Note: Do not force the head down.

BENT-OVER SHOULDER STRETCH

Sit on a chair and interlock your fingers behind the back. Stretch arms, bend over and pull the arms slowly up and over the back.

Cooling Down

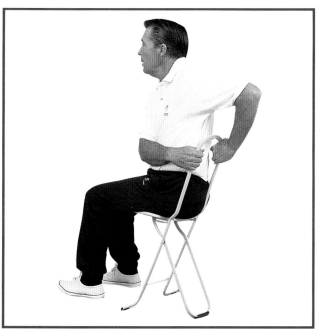

SPINAL TWIST

Sit on a chair and point both feet straight ahead. Slowly turn the upper body around and place both hands at waist-height on the back rest. Hold for eight seconds. Release the grip and turn slowly back to a normal sitting position. Repeat on the opposite side.

LATERAL SHOULDER STRETCH

Crouch on the knees a comfortable distance from a chair. Place both hands on the seat of the chair with arms stretched out. Keep the head between the arms. Push down from the shoulder and feel the latissimus dorsi stretching on the downward movement.

TRUNK TWIST

The flexibility of the spine is very important for the golf swing. Lie on your back and stretch out your arms at shoulder-height on the floor. Bend the legs and bring them up onto the chest. The higher you pull your knees up to your chest, the more you will stretch the spine. Breathe in and turn both legs, with knees bent, towards the side until they make contact with the floor, while keeping your arms and shoulders still on the floor. Breathe out and hold for eight seconds. Breathe in, pull the knees up and return to the original position. Breathe out and relax. Repeat six times, then work the other side.

Note: Do not do this movement with straight legs and keep the knees as close to the chest as possible.

Cooling Down

ELONGATION STRETCH

Lie on your back. Stretch the arms over the head with your legs out straight. Try to reach out as far as is comfortable with both arms and legs. Hold for ten seconds and relax.

SINGLE KNEE-TUCK

The exercise stretches the lower back, the hip extensors and the hamstrings, and helps to prevent injuries in this area. Lie down on your back. Breathe in and pull one knee onto the chest with both hands, keeping the other leg stretched. Bring the head up to meet the knee and breathe out. Hold for eight seconds. Return to the original position and change legs. Repeat six times each side.

CAT STRETCH

Go down on all fours. Keep the back straight. Breathe in. Pull the head in, contract the stomach muscles and round the back as far as is comfortably possible and breathe out. Hold for eight seconds and return to the original position.

Gym Workout

Although many stressed executives flock into the gyms in the early morning hours to stay in shape, as an antidote to their strenuous lives, many golfers appear to be intimidated by gym equipment. Training with machines used to be associated with boxing, weight lifting, body building or football. Professional golfers are only slowly beginning to recognize the benefits of regular gym workouts. Today, a number of players travel with a personal fitness coach and mobile gym while on tour.

Obviously, it doesn't take a great deal of strength to swing a club, but doing so accurately and repeatedly demands both endurance as well as strength. These are exactly the two primary objectives of training with machines.

Training equipment is actually quite versatile. You can increase your strength and stamina working with the same machine. Once you have mastered the exercise, you can add weight to the equipment and do fewer repetitions to build up strength, or you add repetitions with very little weight to boost your endurance.

Working out with machines is the only way to stretch the muscles to the maximum at all possible angles of the joints. This is achieved by attaching a limb to the machine by way of a cam or rolling levers. There are machines for almost every type of movement.

However, the key to success is regularity. If you don't have equipment at home or in the office, if there is no gym in your neighbourhood, and you don't spend a lot of time in hotels with gyms, forget it. You won't benefit from the occasional training session.

Before embarking on fitness training in the gym, it is imperative to check with your physician. And if you have never entered a gym before, talk to the trainer first. He will show you all the exercises you can do with the available equipment. Explain to him what you intend to work on, and take along the results of our fitness test. The trainer may want to put you through a different programme and will suggest a personal training schedule for you based on the machines which are available.

Remember what I said about power training earlier in this book. Start with low resistance levels of about two to five pounds. As you progress, you may slowly add up to ten or 15 pounds to work on your power, but keep repetitions down. You don't want to end up with bulging muscles which get in the way of your golf swing.

To work on your endurance level, stick to a light weight and gradually increase repetitions to 50, 100 or even several hundred as I do.

Train a maximum of three times a week, and don't forget to warm-up and stretch first. Cool down afterwards with easy warm-up and stretching exercises after every session.

You don't need to be a super-athlete, but neither should you be totally unfit to

Gym Workout

follow this routine which you can use to substitute the corresponding optional exercises from the power and calisthenics categories. The exercises should be done in the sequence I describe them to train the big muscles before the small ones. This will help you to keep the injury risk down.

STATIONARY BICYCLE

I begin my workout on the exercycle. I pedal for about 25 minutes to work up a good sweat. When you start, don't discourage yourself by setting the tension on the cycle so high that you are winded within minutes. Set the tension low so you can go for longer. What you want to do is to get the heart pumping vigorously. Start with ten minutes and as you get fitter increase both time and tension, so that you're strengthening the legs as well.

LEG EXTENSION

From a seated position you place your foot under the bar and extend your leg to raise the appropriate weight. You will feel the tension in your quadriceps, the largest muscles in the front of the thigh. You must control the lifting and lowering of the weight for the maximum benefit. Repeat ten times and work alternate legs.

LEG CURL

Lying on your stomach, this is effectively the reverse of the previous exercise to work those muscles at the back of the thigh, the hamstrings. Place the back of your heels under the pad with the appropriate weight and lift the pad all the way up to your buttocks. Repeat ten times.

CALF RAISE

In a standing position, place the front of the feet on a raised platform or block with weights on your hands or shoulders. Lift your heels up as high as you can while standing on your toes and return to the original position. With toes facing forward you will work the middle calves, with toes facing inwards the outer calves, and with toes facing outwards the inner calves. Repeat ten times.

LATERAL PULL-DOWN

This works the biggest muscle in your back, the latissimus dorsi. In a seated position, keeping your back straight and the stomach tucked in, raise both hands up above your head and hold the bar handles. Pull down the bar to the neck and then release slowly back to the starting position. Breathe out as you pull down and breathe in as you release. Repeat ten times.

ROWING MACHINE

In a seated position, with knees bent, stretch out the arms and grasp the pulley handles. Pull back elbows as far as you can in a rowing motion and then go back to the starting position in a controlled manner. Repeat 20 times.

SIT-UP WITH WEIGHTS

This is the box standard sit up exercise which you will be familiar with. Holding a weight in both hands at your chest makes it a bit tougher – but the benefits will be obvious as you persevere. Repeat 20 times.

HAND EXERCISE WITH WEIGHTS

To strengthen your wrists, fingers and muscles in the hand take a dumbbell in one hand. From a seated position rest the hand with the dumbbell on the knee and grasp the wrist with the other hand. Lift the dumbbell up and down as far as your wrist will go. Alternate with the other hand.

STAIR MACHINE

This is an aerobic exercise machine for the training of your cardiovascular system, and at the same time it is great for the lower body and legs. It is an ideal warm up and cool down exercise prior to and after exercise. Supplement this by walking up stairs instead of using escalators whenever you have the opportunity.

BACK EXTENSION WITH WEIGHTS

This admittedly looks a bit like a torture instrument, but it is wonderful for the lower back. Sit on the machine and put your heels under the restraint pad, making sure your hips rest right on the support pad. Let your body hang loose, and with hands across your chest and stomach tucked in firmly, bend backwards until you are parallel to the floor, but no further. Then return to the starting position. Be careful with this exercise if you have any back problems.

Swing Clinic

Technique is only as good as your muscle memory since your mind must be free to focus on the strategic planning of the game. To train your muscles to build up that memory you should practise regularly these swing exercises.

This workout will also assist you in getting a feel for the components of the swing and to correct ingrained swing faults. You won't even need to go to the driving range to do most of them.

HALF SWING

Working on your half swing will help you to monitor the correct backswing and followthrough just before and after impact. If you master the half swing you will deliver the club with much more accuracy and power at impact.

Place one club in front of, and another behind the ball, in line with the target. Put a third club in front of your feet parallel to the others. Place a fourth club at right angles to the third club right between your feet opposite the ball.

Take any club from a sand wedge up to a 7-iron, grip the club down and bend your knees a little more than

usual. Take a backswing with a straight left arm no more than hip-high. A reverse turn of the left forearm moves the clubface back into a square position at impact.

After impact the right straight arm starts to roll over the left arm until you get into same hip-high position as on the backswing. Keep the head in line with the ball, using the spine as a vertical axis, turning shoulders and hips by lifting the right heel off the ground and turning the right instep inwards. Weight transfers to the left foot. The club shaft is parallel to the ground and to the target line. Your belt buckle and hands should be in line. If you have done it correctly you should be able to see your left palm and the ball should fly higher and roll less than after a chip shot with the same club. Repeat 50 times. Without a ball this exercise is suitable for home and office-use.

FULL SWING

To check your alignment for the full swing, use the same set-up as for the half swing. Place one club in front of and another behind the ball in line with the target. Put a third club in front of your feet, parallel to the others. Place a fourth club at right angles to the third club right between your feet opposite the ball.

Turn your hips and

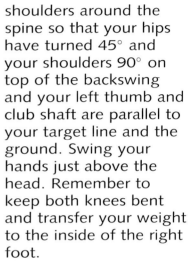
Swing Clinic

shoulders around the spine so that your hips have turned 45° and your shoulders 90° on top of the backswing and your left thumb and club shaft are parallel to your target line and the ground. Swing your hands just above the head. Remember to keep both knees bent and transfer your weight to the inside of the right foot.

Swing the club into impact by reversing the backswing. At the follow-through the hands finish with a firm grip head-high. Visualize your ideal finish position and swing your hands into this finish position like you would park your car in the garage. The left wrist remains in a straight line with the forearm and the back of the left hand. The left forearm acts as an upright support for the club. Your belt buckle and body are facing parallel towards the target. Your weight has been transferred to the outside of the left foot.

BEACHBALL SWING

This exercise will help you to get a feel for the swing and also boost your visualization which forms an important part of course strategy as we will see in the chapter on mental fitness. Choose a colour of your beachball which is pointing upwards during your address position (red in our picture). In your half swing the chosen colour is pointing upwards in the backswing and in the finishing position. Repeat until you get it right 20 times in a row.

ONE-ARM-SWING

Swinging with only one arm has as much to do with feel and control as with coordination. Just watch what happens to your golf swing when you do it left-handed and left-handed only for the first time! Swing the club with your straight left arm backwards and forwards along the target line by turning your left forearm so that the left thumb is parallel to the ground on top of the backswing and follow-through. Practise until this movement resembles your normal swing. Repeat with your right arm.

TEE-TO-TEE EXERCISE

Many golfers find it difficult to practise the correct turn of the left forearm and finding the right club path. Here is the remedy. Place a tee into the top of the club grip of your 8-iron. Tee up a ball. Swing hands back while turning the left forearm until the tee in the grip points towards the teed-up ball. After hitting the ball by turning the left forearm into the follow-through, end up with the tee inserted in the club grip pointing towards the spot where the ball was teed up. Repeat 20 times. If you leave the ball in the bag, you can even do this exercise on your lawn.

129

PIVOT

This exercise focuses entirely on the correct shoulder turn. Again, it reminds your muscles and ligaments of what they are supposed to do. It also teaches you how it is supposed to feel. Criss-cross your arms in front of your chest, place your right hand on the left shoulder and your left hand on the right shoulder. Turn your shoulders on a horizontal plane around your spine during the full swing. You need to keep in mind to initiate the backswing by rotating the hip backwards by about 45°. At the top of the backswing your shoulders must turn 90° each side. Do 20 times.

Swing Clinic

SCALE TEST

This exercise allows you to check your weight distribution on top of your backswing and follow-through. All you need is two bathroom scales and a place where you can perform a full swing with a club. Your weight distribution on top of the backswing should be approximately 70 per cent on the right foot and 30 per cent on the left. In the finishing position the scales should show 90 per cent of your weight on the left foot and ten per cent on the right.

Preplay Routine

Quite a number of amateur golfers appear to think that they can rush up from their desks to the first tee, arriving breathlessly within minutes of their tee-off-time, still tucking their shirt into their pants. What results is a bad round, or worse, a torn ligament or back problem.

The golf swing is a relatively quick movement that requires good muscle coordination. You must take the time to warm up and stretch the relevant muscle group before you belt away at the ball. This is especially true if you don't exercise regularly.

The eight exercises you will find on the following pages are designed as a quick fix before the round to limber you up and prevent injuries. They are by no means a substitute for the exercise routine featured earlier in this book. The exercises are described in the order you should do them, and you should do them all. There are no options. Allow 15 to 20 minutes for the exercises which will also give your mind a chance to get attuned to the game.

HEAD TURN

Turn your head from side to side while keeping the chin up and looking straight ahead. Stretch as much as possible. Repeat five times each side.

CLUB LIFT

Place a club on the ground in front of you, parallel to your feet. Stand straight, the feet shoulder-width apart, with slightly bent knees. Pick the club up with stretched arms by bending forward from the hip. Lift the club over and behind your head and reverse the movement until the club is on the ground again. Repeat five times.

Preplay Routine

CLUB TILT

Hold a club with straight arms above your head with your feet hip-wide apart. Bend sideways left and right. Keep the back straight. Repeat five times.

TORSO TWIST

Stand again upright in
the same position as
before, holding a club
behind the neck and
across the shoulders.
Twist your torso left and
right, but keep the
shoulders straight.
Repeat ten times.

BACK STRETCH WITH CLUB

From the same position, take a club as support placing the clubhead about one yard in front of you on the ground. Straighten your arms and stretch your back parallel to the ground. Don't curve your spine. Count to ten while holding this position. Repeat five times.

SLALOM

This is my version of summer ski. Stand upright, knees bent, feet together and use two golf clubs as supporting ski poles in each hand. With the clubs firmly grounded, jump as far to the left and to the right as you can by turning the body from the hips. Keep the feet together as if to avoid slalom obstacles. Start slowly. Repeat ten times each side.

Preplay Routine

BACKWARD LUNGE

Hold on to your ski poles, you will need them again. Ground the clubs slightly ahead of your feet left and right. Step back with your right foot as far as possible without resting the knee on the ground. Your back should remain fairly straight and your left knee bent into a right angle. Repeat five times on each leg.

TWO-CLUB-SWING

Grip two clubs together and start swinging very slowly while trying to imitate your normal swing path as closely as possible. Repeat ten times. Increase speed and do another ten.

Injury Prevention

There are doctors who claim that golf is bad for your back. Let me put this opinion into perspective. If statistics are to be believed, 200 million people in the world suffer from lower back pain. But there are only 50 million golfers in the world, not all of whom have back injuries. The conclusion is that the human spine is a very vulnerable part of the body which tends to get hurt a lot if not properly protected. Today's lifestyle, a lack of regular exercise, slouching in armchairs, driving in cars for long hours and working in offices where the furniture is not ergonomically designed for maximum lumbar support puts tremendous strain on the vertebra.

Having said that, it is true that back pain is, indeed, the most frequent complaint of golfers. I have suffered from it myself at one stage.

Lower back pains are like most golf-related health problems, compounded over time. They usually are the result of a combination of factors – a wrong stance, bad posture, poor golf swing mechanics and untrained muscles in the back and abdomen. Bad habits on the course while teeing up, putting and holing out, add to the pressure on the spine.

You should always bend your knees, not your back, when teeing up, lining up a putt or holing out. When you practise putting over a long period of time take a break and do some of the limbering exercises you will find below. You can also squeeze in some of these while waiting for other players to tee off during a round.

Fortunately, acute, traumatic injuries from golf are rare. But ingrained swing faults, teeing-off without proper warm-up, and whacking at the ball to gain extra yardage without regular training can also lead to injuries of shoulders, elbows and knees.

There is only one way to prevent injuries on the golf course and that is regular exercise. Your routine must cover stretching, calisthenics and the power programme to protect your body best. There are no short-cuts. That is how I got rid of my back pain.

I do a lot of heel drops. You need to stand on a step of a stair, feet together, on your toes. Slowly let your heels drop below the toes. This stretches the muscles in the entire back and legs and prevents muscle spasms.

The exercises you find below are specifically designed to prevent golf injuries with special emphasis on stretching and strengthening the back muscles. You can do them easily on the range or out on the course whenever you feel slightly uncomfortable. They are by no means a substitute for a regular fitness training, nor are they designed to cure back aches.

FORWARD BEND

Stand upright with your legs about shoulder-wide apart, knees slightly bent. Lean forward from the hips and let your arms dangle down while shaking them to loosen the shoulders.

HULA

To alleviate pain in the lower back, stand upright, feet shoulder-wide apart, knees slightly bent, hands resting on your hips. Do a hula-hula dance by rotating the hips. Repeat 20 times each way.

147

HIP BEND

Stand upright, feet shoulder-wide apart, knees slightly bent. Bend from the hip forward, letting your arms dangle down. Lift your upper body, place your hands in the small of your back and bend backwards. Repeat until the tension in the muscles is eased.

WRIST CIRCLES

Stand comfortably. Interlock your fingers and circle your wrists. Repeat ten times each, clockwise and anti-clockwise.

ARM STRETCH

Stand comfortably and
interlock your fingers.
Stretch and raise your
arms in front of you so
that the back of the
hands is facing you.

Travel with Ease

Both amateur golfers and professionals are frequently on the road, and neither is the better for it. Stress, dehydration, jet lag, sea sickness and headaches rank high on any frequent flyer's complaint list. In fact, 99.9 per cent of all passengers appear to suffer from long-haul flights. Having spent over eight million airborne miles I have devised my own survival suitcase.

In it went a lot of vitamin C and even sleeping pills, until I discovered the Anti-Jet-Lag Formula manufactured by American Biosearch of San Diego. Besides Vitamins C and B_6 these tablets contain two natural amino acids. The scientists at American Biosearch have told me that our bodies use one amino acid, derived from protein, during the day to stimulate wakefulness, and the other, derived from carbohydrate, in the evening to promote sleep. Taking the daytime tablets in the morning and at lunch, and the bedtime tablets before retiring helps me and you adjust to the new zone.

Another item I always slip into my case is an inflatable pillow for neck support. This is important as I spend most of my time on planes asleep. I set my watch on arrival time, even before the plane takes off. I sometimes also try to rest less before the trip to adjust to the new time zone at destination and ensure that I sleep on the plane.

I seldom watch inflight videos or listen to music. I tell the flight attendant that I don't want to be disturbed, take an eye shade out of my survival case, and go to sleep. Unfortunately, I'm not allowed to sleep on the floor. Nothing rivals the horizontal position to give the body, especially the back, a good night's rest. I know from experience that a golfer's back is prone to wear and tear, and keeping it as straight as possible as often as I can has helped me cope with strain and injuries.

If I don't sleep, I exercise. Confined to such a small place, without much room to shift position, people frequently suffer from muscle aches and cramps. To prevent these, stretching is the best you can do. Stand up and do as much stretching as you can, especially stretch your neck before going to sleep. Pull your knees up and through to your stomach, then stretch your legs out straight, place them under the seat in front of you and push upwards.

Isometric exercises can also do you a lot of good. You can sit in the seat and put your hands on your legs and try to push your legs up while resisting with your hands. That's a great stomach exercise. Or go forward on your left knee and stretch your right leg and then go forward on your right leg and stretch your left leg as far as possible. You can even do sit-ups in the aisle, which is what I usually do when they put the lights out.

On aircraft most people indulge in the first class food fare that airlines pamper their passengers with these days. They drink too much alcohol, eat the wrong things, and some even smoke. I would hate to arrive feeling as dreadful as many of them must feel.

As it is, the stomach is already struggling throughout air pockets and turbulence while trying to adjust to new hours. On arrival, the foreign and exotic menus will bewilder it further. Why don't you give it an easy time while you can? Your stomach is best able to adjust to changes if it has nothing to digest at all. Fasting is the best possible favour you can do it.

If you must eat, eat fruit. Fresh or dried fruit is one of the items I often take onboard. If you need something more substantial, at least make it high fiber, like a good whole grain bread. I try to have as little to eat as possible – fruit, salads, fish, pasta, lots of water, juices, no alcohol and no animal fats. If you dread jet lag, stay away from heavy foods, red meat and junk food. Drink lots of water, as you can easily become dehydrated in the pressurized cabin.

Upon arrival, you must pretend that it's just another normal working day and adjust to the local time at once. When I get to my hotel I start off by soaking in a hot tub, followed by a cold shower to get the circulation going. Believe me, you'll get used to the cold showers and feel the benefits! I then head straight for the golf course and practise. Fresh air and exercise will get you back in shape as well.

A good walk, your workout programme, or a massage is probably all you need to alert body and mind to the day ahead. By the time you go to bed, you want to be tired from a day well spent, so that you can sleep easily and soundly. The first night's sleep is essential.

That evening I will have a meal which is high on carbohydrates and low on protein, such as pasta with vegetables, to enhance the effect of the anti-jet-lag tablets. I also make sure I get plenty of roughage. My breakfast usually includes all-bran cereal, prunes or other fruit. This is especially important for the first couple of days, to help your stomach over the adjustments.

The above may appear a sizeable list of things to keep in mind and in your own survival suitcase, just to arrive in shape. But remember, if you travel as I do, you will always travel well.

Mental Fitness

Golf is essentially a game of the mind. Just think about it. You can hit a great shot, and still land in trouble, you can have a good round and still lose. You have no team partner to get you out of a bad lie. You have to contend with the conditions of the course, the weather, the grass. You must fight boredom, frustration, anger and stress. And you have all of two and a half minutes to regain your composure before your next shot.

Fortunately, the brain, which accounts for as much as 80 per cent of our performance on the golf course, can be trained as well as the muscles, although few golfers make the effort to do so. If they were to equal or surpass all the hours they spend on the driving range perfecting their physical skills by exercising their mental abilities, the results would be astounding.

ATTITUDE

Since the mind shapes the action, you need to approach your game with a positive mental attitude. You have already laid the foundation for greater confidence on the course by practising your technical skills, by building up your muscles through exercises, and by getting in shape through a good diet. Now you must learn to control your thoughts.

A lot of players hack their way across a golf course while telling themselves they always drive into the rough or out of bounds on this hole, land in the bunker on that hole, and that they have missed exactly this same short putt only last week. They are convinced that they will remain poor golfers to the end of their days, and proceed to droop head and shoulders, assuming a negative posture to demonstrate to everybody who watches that this is in fact true. Naturally their score tallies with this attitude.

It seems people ruminate in their minds about past mistakes and failures more often than about past successes, but we can decide to be the masters of our thoughts if we make up our minds to do so.

Let me give you an example. When I was a young professional and absolutely nowhere on the international circuit, I used to stand in front of my mirror and say to my reflection in the glass, 'you are the world's greatest golfer'. I did that over and over again, although it was not true.

Did you ever hear of people talking themselves out of headaches by repeating ever so often that they are feeling better and better and better? And eventually their body adjusts, just as the body adjusts to thoughts of putting or driving badly if you just put your mind to it. There is no power as great as the power of your mind. You can make the best or the worst of it – it's entirely up to you.

The secret of success is to ban every negative thought from your mind and every memory of a bad shot. I know it's not easy, because I have worked hard to turn my negative habits into positive ones. When I am asked how I play, I say regardless of my score, 'better than ever in my life'. For who else will cheer me on if I don't? And if nobody does, I will certainly play worse.

Don't let anybody talk you down. If someone reminds me of a few missed putts after a round, I always will point out to him the marvellous putts on the 7th or 9th hole. We all are bound to make mistakes sometimes. Let's count our blessings if we don't make mistakes all the time.

If you make a blunder, smile and keep your head high and have a good laugh at yourself. Always remember, even top professionals play less than ten great shots during a round of, say, 62. And if you manage one great shot, celebrate! Reward your success and you will be well on your way to more.

Create a success history. Put pen to paper and list all your past victories be they third place in a monthly medal, runner-up in a club championship or the five dollars you won from John Smith last Saturday. Are you impressed? I bet you are. Keep your list and fill it further as you go along. You will soon wonder why you ever considered yourself a lousy golfer.

STRATEGY

Out on the course, you always have to do your best. It doesn't matter whether you win or lose, as long as you make

CHECKLIST

- Talk yourself into being a good golfer

- Ban negative thoughts from your mind

- Forget the bad shots

- Don't let others talk you down

- Laugh at your blunders

- Keep your head high when you play

- Reward your success

- Write down your history of success

every shot count. Don't think of the last shot, however good or bad it may have been and don't think of the one three holes down the road. Focus on the one you're facing now. Concentrate on the ball during the swing, reading the wording or focusing on the logo, and give it your best shot. Winners don't give any single stroke away regardless of their score.

If your ball lands in a divot, disappears in deep rough or sails out of bounds, don't grumble. After all, everybody else plays that same course in those same conditions and gets frustrated, too. Enjoy the challenge to your skills and your will power. Learn from the champions. They thrive on adversity.

Whatever happens, stick to your pre-shot routine. Analyze the lie of the ball, take stock of the pin position, the hazards, the terrain, watch the wind, consider the height of the location, the dryness and type of grass, determine the line of flight, the kind of shot you want to make, check the distance and choose your club. Once you have decided on the stroke and the club, don't change.

Visualize the exact shot you aim for, visualize your swing, imagine you hear the contact on the ball, and follow in your mind the flight. See the ball drop where you want it to drop. Watch it roll, and enjoy your success. Then play the shot. And if you know the distance of your clubs and the level of your skills you will be rewarded.

Don't, however, rush to the next tee. You will only swing faster than normal,

mishit the ball and lose your tempo.
Maintain your rhythm while walking on
the course. Since I don't want to talk on
the course between the shots, I keep my
pace by measuring the length of my shot,
or by enjoying the birds and the scenery
or by just thinking of nothing at all.

A leisurely pace on the course also
ensures that you stay relaxed. Nobody
has mastered the art of deliberate slow
motion under stress better than Bobby
Locke. He could tie his shoe-laces with
the studied precision, control and pace of
a neuro-surgeon at work. On the golf
course, he would invariably drive his
playing partners, including myself, to
distraction while he remained perfectly
relaxed and went on to claim the trophy
in an equally leisurely manner.

IMPROVE YOUR GAME

Before you can start using your brain to
improve your game you need to sit down
and take stock. Arm yourself with pen and
paper and fill out the list below. Be honest
and precise. It won't do for you to *hope* to
reduce your handicap. You must write
down your current handicap and the one
you hope to achieve and when you want
to achieve it. Consider how much time are
you able and willing to spend on
improving the game? How quickly did
your handicap reduce previously?

Determine your short-term goals. What
are your weaknesses? Are they confined
to certain clubs? Which? Let's say you

CHECKLIST

- Always do your best

- Play one shot at a time

- Never quit on a shot

- Accept adversity

- Maintain your pre-shot routine

- Stick to the shot and club you have selected

- Visualize your shot

- Maintain your tempo

hook your drive. How many straight drives do you manage during a round? How many do you manage on the practice ground? How many straight drives out of how many practice shots do you aim for within the next month? You have to know your past record and present level to start with.

Make sure that your goals are realistic and measurable. They must not be so high that you can't reach them nor so low that you get bored. How well do you really want to play? Stick to your goal.

PRACTICE PLAN

Long-Term Goals

Current handicap:

Target handicap:

Time frame:

Practice hours per week:

Playing hours per week:

Short-Term Goals

Current weakness:

Occurrence on course per round:

Occurrence on driving range per hour:

Target occurrence on driving range:

Time frame:

Practice hours per week for this target:

Out on the driving range, visualization can do as much for you as it does on the course, if not more. Instead of belting away ball after ball with the same club in quick succession, imagine you are playing your home course. Start with the driver. Tee up the ball. Imagine your first hole. Pick your target area, follow your usual pre-shot routine, then fire away.

Imagine yourself walking down the first fairway to where your ball would have landed. Take a break of a minute or so to get closer to the real course conditions. Select the club for your next shot, follow your pre-shot routine and continue playing your course in your mind.

Another good exercise for the driving range is to concentrate on individual muscle groups, for instance your fingers, during the swing. Describe how they feel until you get a very concrete picture of what is happening to all the parts of your body during the swing.

Try hitting balls with closed eyes. You will probably find that your swing gets smoother because you are not distracted from the action and you will be much more relaxed. There is nothing like it to gain feel. This practice helps on the putting green as well.

I often work on my putting at home in a comfortable armchair. I close my eyes and imagine myself on a practice green with two balls. I'll tell myself the feel of the stroke I want and in my mind set up for it. I feel my putter grip in my hand and practise the type of putt I've had trouble with. I picture the line of the roll of each ball and hear it drop into the cup. This, of course, is also a good practice for any other problems I may have with certain shots or part of my swing.

Whenever I walk away from the 18th green, I start replaying the round in my mind, shot by shot. I try to realize where I've made mistakes and learn from them. Then, I'll go on to working on my game plan for the next day and rehearse how I'm going to play each hole, each shot.

STRESS CONTROL

It is easy to get frustrated on the golf course. A drive lands in a divot, an approach shoots out of bound, a long iron shot lands in the water, the putting line was misread, the grass is faster or slower than we thought, we lose swing and tempo and feel like throwing the clubs away and walking home.

The temptation is great to blame others for one's poor performance. A spectator who coughs, a caddie who is slow or a playing partner who doesn't stop talking. However, anger is self-defeating. Whenever I get irritable or upset, I find it works wonders to lie down either physically or just in my mind. You can't shout if you lie down. Try it. You can't but relax. After the round, head for the nearest pool. Swimming soothes body and soul.

In a tournament, whether it's your weekly foursome or the U.S. Masters, the stress is often too much for the players.

162

Mental Fitness

Confidence and calm appear to all have been left in the locker-room. But you can do better than that. Come well prepared. Check the course out first, know your current skill level well, and do your exercise programme and your routine on the driving range. All this will give you confidence.

After the first tee, forget about your opponents. And don't lose your normal timing. Focus on one shot at a time, and should it land in the ditch, remember that everybody else fires unlucky shots as well. You get plenty of strokes for the round, so one bogey or double bogey is not the end of the tournament.

I reckon, a scratch player can expect about five good shots per round, two chip shots, a bunker shot and two putts. Subsequently, he is entitled to about five bad shots to stay at par. As a handicap golfer, you have the right to make many more mistakes. If you are determined to win, sooner or later you will.

WEIGHT CHART

MEN	
Height	Weight
5'4"	122–145 lbs
5'6"	130–155 lbs
5'8"	139–166 lbs
5'10"	147–174 lbs
6'	154–183 lbs
6'2"	162–192 lbs
6'3"	165–195 lbs

WOMEN	
Height	Weight
5'	100–118 lbs
5'2"	107–125 lbs
5'4"	113–132 lbs
5'6"	120–139 lbs
5'8"	126–146 lbs
5'10"	133–156 lbs
6'	141–166 lbs

Diet for Champions

To become fit for golf you need to complement a solid training programme with a sensible diet. After all, we are what – and how much – we eat. Selecting the right kind and amount of food you need has at least as much impact on your performance as your exercise routine.

People today tend to eat too much. As a rule of thumb, every calorie you feed your body is converted into energy, if you are active, or into body fat, if you are not. A couch potato burns up as little as 1,000 calories a day, an active golfer between 2,000 and 3,500, and a professional weight lifter twice as many.

Strip down, get on your bathroom scale and compare the result with the healthy weight guideline from the American Medical Association. The lower end of the range is for slightly built persons, the upper end for people with large frames.

If you need to lose weight, start by giving your body a rest with one day of fast. Throughout that day you can drink fruit juices and water, and I promise you, you won't starve. Fasting has a marvellous cleansing effect and will help you to break with your eating patterns.

Learn to listen to your body. Don't eat because it's time. Eat because you're hungry. If you're not hungry, don't eat. You will probably find that you – like myself – need only two meals a day with some fruit in between most of the time.

164

Should two meals a day be insufficient for you, eat the most when you are the most active. In other words, follow the old adage: Breakfast like a king, lunch like a prince, and dine like a pauper. If you maintain your fitness programme, and eat reasonable amounts of sensible food at the right time, you can't help losing weight.

You may have read articles about my sipping honey on the course, or eating a handful of raisins on the run, but actually I had little knowledge of nutrition until I turned 30. I used to think – like so many fitness and figure-conscious people – that protein, steak and shrimp were the answer. Nothing is further from the truth. Although proteins are needed to build and repair muscle, an excess may strain liver and kidney and will add to the fat, not the muscles, in your body.

Carbohydrates have been proven in clinical experiments to be the best energy source for athletic activity. Especially marathon runners benefit from a diet high on carbohydrates for several days before the competition. It appears that the body has the ability to store carbohydrates – converted into glycogen – in large quantities improving overall endurance in sports activities lasting more than one hour. But the body needs time to work on it. A quick oat bar before the tournament won't do the trick.

It is generally recognized among physicians today that carbohydrates should supply at least half the calories of a healthy diet, fats about 30 per cent, and

A HEALTHY DIET

EYE OPENER
glass of water, chopped garlic with honey

BREAKFAST
raisin bran cereal with skim milk, banana and strawberries or muesli of raw oats, raisin, banana, nuts, wheat germ, orange juice, yogurt, whole-wheat toast with little butter, herbal tea and honey

LUNCH
sandwich of brown bread with fish, juice, fruit

ON THE GOLF COURSE
whole-wheat sandwich with peanut butter and honey, nuts, raisins, dried fruit, banana

SPECIAL TREAT
no-fat frozen yogurt

DINNER
pasta, fish, chicken or meat, salad with onions, tomatoes and garlic, cabbage, carrots or spinach, fruits

proteins no more than 15 per cent. Mind you, we are talking calories, not grams and pounds. You need to eat very little fat to get a lot of calories, while the reverse is true for protein.

Your daily diet should consist of natural, unprocessed food: pasta, rice or bread, and fresh fruits or slightly cooked vegetables, meat, fish, cheese or milk and nuts. Fats should consist in equal parts of animal and vegetable origin. And don't forget to drink at least a litre a day, water and juices that is.

The preparation of the food is almost as important as the ingredients themselves. Vegetables and fruits should be consumed raw whenever possible. If food has to be cooked, less does less harm to the nutrients. And last but not least, remember that broiling adds less calories to the meal than frying.

These days, many people rush their food while standing in the kitchen, briefcase in hand, gulping down the coffee, and biting off a sandwich on the run to the bus stop. They subsequently are surprised if their digestion gives them problems. Take time to chew your food. This is half the digestion. Your stomach will then also be able to tell you when to stop and prevent you from overeating.

Although my diet of fresh foods looks after my basic vitamin and mineral needs throughout the day, I take supplements. Vitamin E is a must, as it improves the blood circulation and assists in preventing cramps and apart from eggs precious few other foods contain it.

Diet for Champions

Beta Carotene and Vitamin C are needed to grow and repair body tissue and protect the muscles from minor injuries. Vitamin B replenishes energy. Lastly, the mineral Zinc, responsible for the contraction of muscles in the body, needs to be replaced to avoid fatigue, infection and injury.

Don't eat immediately before heading for the golf course or the gym. Your stomach needs at least one and a half hours to cope with a full meal. A rest of two hours is even better to allow the body to gear up for exercise. You will then be in top form.

I have lived with a regimen of natural health food for half a lifetime, but I have not become a slave to it. I love chocolate and ice cream and cannot always stay away from them. If you crave a beer after a round, a piece of pie or a hamburger, there is nothing wrong with that, provided you do so in moderation and burn up the calories.

The Legacy of Gary Player

The ultimate tribute to the life and times of a great man is that he receives his own imperishable place in history for having played a role for which his name will always be remembered.

In golfing terms, such recognition amounts to more than just a colossal tally of victories which symbolize a personal supremacy and excellence by which future generations can judge themselves.

Victories are important, of course, but invariably destined to be overtaken and capped in the fullness of time. There is, however, a different, more permanent kind of distinction which is locked safely in the chronological evolution of the game and therefore can never be threatened.

This then is the manner in which the phenomenon of Gary Player is to be regarded and remembered, because the archives will show that this diminutive South African transformed the traditional concept of the game – or rather the playing of it – so that it was never quite the same again.

It was not, he concluded, merely a pastime in which a natural flair and eye for a ball were the only requirements, and that the best preparation – if any were really needed – was the game itself.

Player held a different view. He perceived it as pure athletics – albeit mechanical in form – but, as such,

168

requiring a regimen of personal training, development, discipline and diet that would be afforded to any other pursuits.

It was not so much dogma, as discovery. And while it was greeted at first with mild ridicule, it produced another, even greater impact which eventually changed the philosophy of the sport. Player prompted a simple but profound alteration of values. In essence, he made it quite clear he was not afraid to be seen actually trying to win. That, after all, was the only reason he prepared and trained so hard.

Not for him, the old-fashioned, game's-the-thing gentleness in which taking part was the only honourable objective. He wanted to win at all costs. He was not ashamed to show it and, while such naked ambition initially surprised the royal and ancient world, it was to become the pattern for others.

In a sense, the Player approach can be said to have played a pivotal part in creating a competitive climate which directly caused the astounding improvements in the standards of play as players of healthy aspirations realized the value of the Player Principle that hard work plus dedication equals success. Or, as he put it more earthly: 'The more I practise, the luckier I get.'

From the moment he took his place among the champions by winning the 1959 Open at Muirfield, Player was to be a relentless force upon the game and an influence far greater than the three British titles, one U.S. Open, three

Masters and two U.S. PGA Championships attributed to him in the record books.

In many ways, he also brought a spiritual dimension to the game. Or rather, he examined the importance of a correct mental attitude and its influence on success. In so doing, he was ridding the game unwittingly of its old perceptions because, at its best, golf is a complete examination of a man – his skills and his character – and Player's own career was to be devoted to the development of both.

In all of this, he was a victim of circumstance. Indeed, his whole life can be seen as a saga of struggle and triumph against the odds. By the time he was nine, his mother had died and there began a solitary existence punctuated by occasional family traumas that served to teach this undersized young boy that in this world he could really only rely on himself.

More than this, those early shocks – the bereavement and a teenage accident in which he broke his back and was bedridden for almost nine months – taught him another enduring principle of life and golf: Play it as it lies – accept what's dealt and make the best of it. Simply forget about what might have been, and continue on.

Curiously, there seemed also to be a deeper missionary motive running parallel to Player's chosen career. He was, after all, a firm believer and made no secret of the Almighty's involvement in his success as though some solemn bargain had been struck between them. It was a zealous

Gary Player

approach that his contemporaries at times found overpowering.

When he won his last Masters in 1978 with a staggering last-round 65 to catch all his young rival napping, he revealed afterwards that he had constantly repeated a prayer throughout the round. Much earlier in his career, he recalled seeing the 'vision' of his name on the 1965 U.S. Open scoreboard long before he triumphed to complete his personal set of four Grand Slam titles.

The public perceived him as a fierce fighter on the golf course, determined to prevail by every justifiable means at his disposal. He likened himself to a boxer climbing into the ring. Consequently, the disparity between what he said and what he did often laid him open to charges of double standards.

He saw no such inconsistency. In any case, he was accustomed to both controversy and criticism. He held a wider significance in the world as one of South Africa's most famous globe-trotting figures. Against the background of apartheid problems in his own country he was made accountable wherever he went.

More than this, there were times when he was subjected to the most intense pressures and, as well, the intolerable burden of trying to play his best golf while being the target for political activists.

His life was threatened in the United States. Police cars patrolled the streets at night where he stayed. In the 1969 PGA at

Dayton, Ohio, demonstrators threw objects at him and he was obliged to play the last round under police escort. Similar treatment awaited him in Australia and in France where he was also the target for anti-apartheid militants.

He could have slipped away from it in the manner of other sportsmen by leaving the country of his birth to set up home elsewhere, thereby offering the world both a disclaimer and condemnation of the regime. But, he refused and, by staying within his beloved South Africa, played more than a peripheral role in its painful but inevitable transformation.

On a purely personal and more tangible level, he has made immense contributions to this change. Next door to his home in Johannesburg, he built a magnificent multi-racial school for local children and set up a trust fund to help the young on a wider scale because he believed that the future of South Africa lies with the education of all its children.

The curious strand running through nearly all his greatest triumphs on the fairways is that each of them had a moment of crisis in which only the perfect match-winning stroke could save him. Indeed, his championship career began with drama and tears when he thought he had thrown the 1959 title at Muirfield away and had to wait all afternoon before he could be sure nobody would catch him.

His first Masters win involved an extraordinary mishap to Arnold Palmer, who needed only par on the last hole for victory and faced a comfortable approach shot from the middle of the fairway to become champion again. Arnie unaccountably bunkered his shot, thinned the recovery to the back of the green to take six and allow Player, watching the drama on television in the clubhouse, to take the green jacket.

His 1968 British Open win at Carnoustie contained one of the greatest strokes of his career when, with Jack Nicklaus closing in, he thrashed a 3-wood over the Spectacles – the bunkers on the left of the 14th fairway – to a green he could not see to set up an eagle three which sealed that title for him.

At Oakland Hills in 1972, his PGA victory will always be remembered for the blind shot he played over trees and a lake guarding the 15th green to secure a birdie on the final day and thwart the opposition.

And his momentous victory in the 1965 World Match Play Championship at Wentworth, when he was five down with nine holes to play against Tony Lema yet revived to defeat him, offered as much testimony to his indomitable spirit as it did to his tireless skill and stamina.

It would be wrong, however, to suggest that Player was the first champion to discover the true importance of commitment in golf. The other great heroes must all have possessed this necessary ingredient in some measure in order to succeed.

But the difference was that Player personified it. He gave it definition and dimension so that others could copy and follow in whatever measure they chose. He built up his physique through a punishing daily exercise routine and invariably took his weight-training equipment as excess baggage wherever he travelled in the world. To this day, when there seems no obvious urgency, he still pursues his daily routine.

He always believed in the value of a sound diet, though at times seemed to take the practice to eccentric lengths – the bananas, the raisins, the peanuts and the African mealie-mealie dishes – all, no doubt, of immense nutritional value at the time but more important because they revealed the lengths to which he would go to succeed.

There is, however, another aspect to this astounding life of Gary Player. His championship career spanned 19 years, second only to Jack Nicklaus, who endured for 24 years. Such longevity will never be witnessed again. The modern champions are shorter-lived. One question, therefore, may at first perplex students of the Player phenomenon.

It is not the obvious one of precisely how Player lasted for so long at the pinnacle of the game. But, rather, why it mattered so much for him to do so for all that time – particularly with all the sacrifice both personal and professional involved. The secret can be traced to Player's own guiding philosophy.

A talent unfulfilled is the greatest waste of all. The duty is to be the best. That too is probably the most important legacy

Gary Player

that Player leaves for future generations –
an unshirkable obligation to pursue talent
to its limit whatever the cost.

MICHAEL McDONNELL

SELECTED BIBLIOGRAPHY

Anderson, Johnny M. 1989. Better Golf – The Mental Approach to Winning. Planet Books. London.

Cooper, Kenneth H. 1990. Aerobics. Bantam. New York.
  – 1991. Kid Fitness. Bantam. New York.
  – 1994. The Antioxident Revolution. Thomas Nelson Publishers. Nashville.

Fine, Alan. 1993. Mind over Golf. BBC Books. London.

Giam, C.K. and Teh, K.C. 1988. Sports Medicine, Exercise and Fitness. PG Publishing. Singapore.

Graham David. 1985. Winning Golf. Golf Digest/Tennis. Trumbull.

Jobe, Frank W. and Schwab, Diane R. 1986. 30 Exercises for Better Golf. Champion Press. Inglewood.

Mindell, Earl. 1985. Earl Mindell's Shaping up with Vitamins. Warner Books. New York.

Peale, Norman Vincent. 1987. Power of Positive Thinking. Simon & Schuster. New York.

Player, Gary. 1962. Play Golf. William Collins. London.
  – 1962. Golf Secrets. Prentice-Hall. Englewood Cliffs.
  – 1967. Positive Golf. McGraw-Hill Book Company. New York.
  – 1972. 395 Golf Lessons. Digest Books. Northfield.
  – with Harris, Norman. 1979. Gary Player on Fitness and Success. World's Work. Kingswood.
  – 1988. Golf Begins at Fifty. Century Hutchinson. London.

Pollard, Ted. 1991. Fit for the Game – Golf. Ward Lock Limited. London.

Tobias, Maxine and Sullivan, John Patrick. 1992. The Complete Stretching Book. Dorling Kindersley. London.